CHOOSING PURPOSEFUL ALIGNMENT

The Messy Middle of Transformation

TRACEY GREENE-WASHINGTON

To Jamilla,
Get to your first Yes!
Tracy Greene-Washington
11-18-20

Choosing Purposeful Alignment: The Messy Middle of Transformation

Tracey Greene-Washington
400 Gilead Rd, Suite 1624
Huntersville, NC 28078
IndigoInnovationGroup.com

In association with:
Elite Online Publishing
63 East 11400 South #230
Sandy, UT 84070
EliteOnlinePublishing.com

Library of Congress Control Number: 2020920425

ISBN: 979-8692309006

Printed in the United States of America

What people are saying about Tracey Greene-Washington and Choosing Purposeful Alignment

"With the vulnerability we know is required in leadership but is often hard to summon, Greene-Washington shares stories, questions, and insights, becoming the visionary healer you need, want, and wish to guide you in your own beautiful surrender. Greene-Washington leads you through thinking and rethinking permission to change, sustaining your own transformation, and the constant vigilance required to make choices leading to purposeful alignment of your actions with your values."

Mebane Rash

CEO

EducationNC/NCCPPR/Reach NC Voices/First Vote NC

"This book is a breath of fresh air, acknowledging and giving words to new ways of knowing that blossom in the fertile ground of people-centered, system change work. Tracey Washington brilliantly lays forth key strategies and tools to grow your leadership by trusting community, asking critical questions, and pushing through the messy middle to transformational change."

Ashley Shelton

Executive Director

Power Coalition for Equity and Justice

"Tracey's experience as a community change agent comes through in her powerful and inspiring stories. She puts forward practical and actionable strategies for all social leaders, novice and well-seasoned alike, to identify and eliminate distractions that can impede the hard work leading systemic social change and not lose ourselves in the process."

Kristy Teskey

Innovation Catalyst

Faster Glass

"My favorite line in this book comes early. It is the line, "I'm not selling anything, ma'am. I wanted to invite you to a meeting about tutoring resources for children in the community." I love it because the simplicity belies the complexity. The statement is both true and untrue.

It reflects the paradox of leadership. In fact, Tracey Greene-Washington was selling something that day. Not something that would require an immediate cash investment, although that might have been the long-term outcome. In the short-term, she was peddling hope.

As one reads this book, it is clear that hope comes at a cost. For the seller, and for the buyer. Guiding us through the realities of those costs, Greene-Washington provides rare insights into the work of community organizers and change makers. The struggle for them is as real as the struggle for the communities they serve. We owe this author a debt of gratitude for bringing light to a struggle that is so often hidden in plain sight."

Anita Brown-Graham
Professor of Public Law and Government,
UNC School of Government
Director, ncIMPACT Initiative

"For the decade that I have known Tracey, she has been a true game-changer. As a colleague and coach, I witnessed firsthand her commitment to self-discovery and mastery, which is only matched by her love of family and community service. Tracey has developed into a lifestyle the disciplined practice of emotional acceptance, deep reflection, personal awareness, strategic communication, and aspirational visioning—the most salient characteristics of transformational leadership.

History may prove that there is no more timely invitation than this one to clarify purpose, align values, and activate our voices to drive complex social change. Indeed, our collective personal transformation may be exactly what is required to transform communities, institutions, and social systems around the globe."

Marcus F. Walton
President and CEO
Grantmakers for Effective Organizations

To my family, to my collective circle of influence,
and to CoThinkk for your forever support.

Take the Purposeful Alignment Survey

Your First Yes....

A valuable resource to help you discover where you are on your journey towards purposeful alignment.

https://www.indigoinnovationgroup.com/purposeful-alignment-quiz

SPARK INNOVATION. CULTIVATE CHANGE.

Take this free survey to get to your first YES!

Table of Contents

THE PROPOSITION

This book is a proposition for all aspiring, new, emerging, and seasoned game changers. You are called to intentionally create and lean in to a new space to grapple with purpose and alignment. It is a call to navigate through the necessary messy middle of change, which is the gap between your current state and your desired purpose. This proposition is grounded in the belief that purposeful alignment is a choice, a tenet, and an important anchor to becoming a transformational leader, or as I like to say, a game changer.

What is a game changer? I pondered this question as I sat in church and listened to our pastor teach a series titled "Game Changer." This life-changing message forced deep contemplation as I reflected on leaders who drive some of the most innovative work to address complex social change. I quickly realized game changers understand it is imperative for them to activate every resource at their disposal to drive transformational change. And what is transformational change? It is the type of change that drives long-term impact and is void of transactional and performative activities meant to create the illusion of strategy and change. Game changers understand they must constantly work to evolve and align their values with their actions, while solidly anchoring their calling and their faith. And they understand they must get proximal to the messy middle.

"You are being called into something bigger than yourself."

The messy middle is the space where the painful, often unspoken work takes place. That work we whisper about to our most trusted confidants. Through the sacred work, which we often do not prioritize, we can achieve greater impact, work-life integration, and the move from success to significance. In this space, the ability to successfully navigate and stand steadily requires asking hard questions. The messy middle summons the ability to drop into deep self-reflection, vulnerability, active listening, patience, transparency, steady urgency, and an unwavering desire to model compassionate leadership. The messy middle is the place where game changers learn to embrace the necessary transformation to be a leader capable of cultivating leaderful organizations, strategic initiatives, and movements to drive complex social change.

The messy middle is a space that can reveal a variety of pain points, truths, solutions, and challenges. It is where disorientation, fear, discomfort, and uncertainty are heightened. In this place, you feel both powerless and powerful. Surviving the messy middle requires you to ask a series of "what if," "what could be possible," and "what work do I need to do" questions in order to reach further. The creation of new narratives means embracing interruption, new practices, and creative narratives towards inevitable transformation. Transitioning through the messy middle forces game changers to examine and interrogate purpose, alignment, and critical choice points while embracing a game changer posture.

This book serves as a tool for you, as a game changer, to rise and make intentional choices as you are called into something bigger than yourself. As you move through the pages, the stories and thoughts may seem familiar. You might find yourself in a moment you can't quite articulate just yet, while in every ounce of your being, you recognize this is a critical inflection point you must boldly face and reimagine. You recognize a critical moment calling you into a role as a positive disruptor in your life. By saying yes to what is possible, you begin to move purposeful alignment from the fringes of your life to the center, as a non-negotiable.

"Purposeful alignment is unwavering clarity regarding your unique assignment or calling."

Purposeful alignment is unwavering clarity regarding your unique assignment or calling in spaces, relationships, initiatives, communities, and institutions. Coupled with the intentional and strategic activation and positioning of your voice, unique gifts, role, and compounded experiences, purposeful alignment allows you to drive momentous change. This positioning enables you to embrace the messy middle of transformation on your journey to impact complex social change in a way you only dreamed of achieving. On this journey to purposeful alignment, you set the stage for a set of choice points that enable you to unapologetically level up and embrace a posture that moves you from being successful to being significant to being transformational.

When choosing purposeful alignment, you make the commitment to move through three intentional choice points:

- Choice 1: Embrace the Power of Permission
- Choice 2: Lean in to Transformation
- Choice 3: Become a Game Changer

Throughout this journey, you shift from a place of disorientation to one of clarity. You understand critical decision-making opportunities influence outcomes and are grounded in the belief that cumulative impacts of small choices can be as significant as the impacts of a single decision. You move from a place of surviving to thriving and from a place of unbalanced to balanced. You move from a place of hesitancy to explicitly naming, exploring, and reimagining a series of first yeses at each iteration of the journey. You create the necessary readiness and momentum to accept the final invitation and the choice to arrive at a significant moment in your journey when you know you are purposefully aligned.

CHOICE 1:

EMBRACE THE POWER OF PERMISSION

Stand strong and persistent,
as in the lyrics of Andra Day's song,
"Rise Up".

THE PRINCIPAL STRUGGLE: REDEFINE PERMISSION AND POWER

The struggle between permission and power is not yours to own.

Permission is such a complicated word. It is loaded with images, feelings, fears, and stories of moments throughout your life when you either had to ask for permission, were granted permission, were denied permission, or didn't wait for permission. Each of these unique stories conjures up pivotal memories that helped shape your perception of, and relationship with, permission.

Consequently, permission reveals a continuous loop of spoken and unspoken conversations, internal tensions, and struggles manifested externally as discomfort, uncertainty, and resistance to moments of surrendering, resolve, and celebration. That continuous loop reveals the principal struggle with the traditional definition of permission, which often includes consent, authorization, and power as a right or authority given or delegated to a person or body.

This principal struggle within, between permission and power, necessitates the space to pause and grapple with the realization that the struggle between permission and power is not yours to own. It has no place within your relationships. It is yours to dismantle and redefine. This single realization has the power to set in motion a domino effect of powerful questions to reveal blind spots and interrogate the very idea of who is entitled to give permission, who can receive it, who should honor it, or who can take it away. Meanwhile, you explore the unique role of power in this complex dance. As a result, you redefine the very idea of permission.

Two of my most vivid memories of these lessons are of myself as a community organizer at the very beginning of my career in high school, and in the later part of my career as a seasoned change agent as the founder of CoThinkk, a social change philanthropy. By the time I had matured in my career, I had developed an evolved lens through which to view the power of permission. I had encountered countless lessons, bumps and bruises, and celebrations. Each of these experiences offered me enormous growth and continued evolution.

* * *

HOW IT ALL BEGAN

On a brisk Saturday morning in March, I walked door to door, sharing flyers and inviting community residents to convene to discuss tutoring and how it could impact children in the community. As I arrived at each door, I waited anxiously and with curiosity to see who would answer. At one home, I was met by a beautiful, cocoa-bean-colored woman, who remarked, "What are you selling, because I am not buying today!"

Taking a deep breath, I responded, "I'm not selling anything, ma'am. I wanted to invite you to a meeting about tutoring resources for children in the community." I held out the flyer so she could read it, but I could tell she wasn't quite ready to commit to attending. As she reached out to accept the flyer, I took that gesture as an agreement of interest and silently hoped I would see her there.

The night of the meeting, I arrived early at the community center with two other youth tutors, who I had recruited. We turned on all the lights and the heat and arranged thirty chairs to make room for what I was sure would be a packed house, given all the flyers I had handed out. I had also purchased snacks and beverages to entice people to stay for the entire meeting. We were all set up and ready for the crowd. We waited. And we waited some more. For over an hour, we sat in the community center, which was usually buzzing with families, children, and staff, and we ended up the only ones in attendance. That didn't make it much of a meeting at all. One of the volunteers looked at me and said,

"I guess it's just the three of us. What's your game plan now?" I was disappointed and devastated.

Seeing this beautiful moment forever colored my lens about the importance of asking permission.

The following week, I met with the local NAACP president to discuss my failed meeting attempt. I wanted to know what else I could have done to encourage people to come. Had there been another community meeting scheduled at the same time at another location? Had some sort of incident claimed the attention of the residents? Not for a second did it cross my mind that I had missed some critical steps in preparing for this meeting.

"Did you sit at the table of the community elder and break bread with her?" asked the NAACP president. It seemed like a simple question, but it left me perplexed. "Did you ask her permission and wait for her to make the ask of community residents to come to the meeting?"

These seemed like common-sense actions, but I had overlooked them. Honestly, I had resisted asking for help or permission because I didn't know the impact of such respect and authenticity. At that moment, I realized I had a lot to learn about community organizing. And I immediately renewed my commitment to improve. During those early years, I did not understand the importance of this unspoken protocol in communities. It didn't take me long, however, to learn this most respectful approach to community organizing.

I regrouped and followed the directives of the NAACP president, who was gracious enough to make the introductions and vouch for me. A month later, I sat with a group of elders at a kitchen table, and I broke bread with them. Over homemade lemon pound cake and vanilla ice cream, they began the conversation by asking, "Who are your people?" When I told them I hailed from the Smiths, the Lees, and the Greenes—

that's Greene with an "e"—I felt as if they were thumbing through a mental directory to make connections with my relatives and ancestors, who they might have at one time encountered.

"Oh, I know your grandmother," one woman said with a smile. "She taught preschool." For some reason, I felt relieved, almost as if these elders would now believe I was a real person, someone with roots, someone who cared for their community.

"Yes, ma'am," I replied. "She used to live on Grail Street," I added for further confirmation.

With that, the conversation switched from cautious to a meaty discussion about their strategy to approach parents and mobilize the community. As it turned out, they were all in for the project I desperately wanted to get off the ground. As I cleaned my plate, I attentively listened to their concerns and ideas. Their enthusiasm warmed my heart. Watching their excited faces, I felt like I was in a scene from a movie. These elders knew their community and how to impact people to make change happen. The ideas flowed like a waterfall, and I took notes frantically. At that moment, I realized I didn't need to have all the answers. By the time I pulled away from that tiny kitchen table, I felt unstoppable. I knew my second effort to gather the community would be a success.

Two weeks later, when I arrived at the community center, the experience was completely different. This time, the community room quickly filled with the chatter of women of all shades and shapes, children being settled down, and elders greeting everyone as we called the meeting to order. Seeing this beautiful moment forever colored my lens about the importance of asking permission.

My second experience at the community center also revealed four important lessons:

1. Respecting others enough to ask for permission is about collectively sharing and building power to arrive at shared solutions.

2. Permission is not about powering over others to force them to beg of you or you begging.
3. The traditional view of permission must be interrogated, discarded, and reimagined for greater impact with the understanding that permission does not necessitate waiting and asking for someone else to grant it; this is about the collective.
4. In this very personal, very intimate work of engaging with communities to make critical change, permission is really about respect. Respecting everyone's position and opinion, respecting the knowledge and experience of relationships built over years and generations, and respecting the connection people have to a place and to the outcome being created is vital.

SEASONED AND PUSHING THE ENVELOPE

Learning these simple lessons ignited a deep-seated understanding that has followed me throughout my life and has created a level of ongoing tension in spaces that adhere to the more traditional definition of permission. These lessons were revealed, over and over, throughout the course of my journey in the philanthropic sector. There, I navigated a more traditional perspective of power and permission while grappling with the intentional act of holding up my evolved lens and collective action. All the while, I worked to address systemic issues and serve as a bridger, a provocateur, a capacity-builder, a strategic thought partner, and a network weaver to evolve the sector. This evolution set the stage for the inception of CoThinkk and the deployment of important tools, capacities, relationships, and resources gathered over the course of my career in service to playing a critical role in the ecosystem of change in my home community.

CoThinkk was birthed from witnessing the amazing work led by leaders of color, in Asheville and Western North Carolina, who tackled some of the most challenging and nuanced social issues impacting our region. After engaging in conversation after conversation, as a program officer with a statewide foundation, I could see leaders of color boldly leaning into the hard work of change, challenging the norm, and resisting the urge to wait for others to make room. I was inspired, excited, grateful, and humbled.

Could this be the moment I'd been waiting for since I was a young organizer? Was it finally time to come home? Was this the moment when all the puzzle pieces were positioned in just the right places to facilitate lasting transformational change and impact? Was this an indicator that I could come home to play my role and amplify the amazing work emerging across the region? I stepped back with an intentional pause and realized this was that unique moment when all the pieces aligned just right. There were countless groups investing in and committing to racial equity training, and the momentum and strength and amazing courage from leaders of color shone through. At the same time, I faced the reality that their efforts were under-resourced, lacking visibility, and condemned to silos. They needed an intentional platform to showcase some of the most powerful, innovative, and future-focused solutions to social change. I faced the hard truth that, even in my role, I could only support a small number of these efforts through funding. Unfortunately, many local philanthropic institutions lacked the funding mechanism to support this type of work and had limited understanding of the return on investment for doing so.

Consequently, CoThinkk was designed from its very inception to embody the intention to drive systems change and focus on racial equity. Its very design was carefully crafted to harness and manifest power, permission, and collaboration from a place of centering those most impacted, honoring their voices, and offering gratitude to the countless leaders upon whose shoulders we stood to do this work. We designed CoThinkk to create autonomy, to reimagine and interrupt systems and practices of business as usual, and to serve as a hub of innovation. At its core, CoThinkk was formed to consistently interrupt and disrupt the carefully orchestrated rhythm of systems that serve as barriers for thriving communities.

CoThinkk was founded on the principles of social change philanthropy and birthed out a proposition of what could be possible if we collectively create supportive networks, accelerate change, and seed new initiatives to address the most vexing social issues facing communities of color in Asheville and the region. As an innovative model anchored in shifting mental models, centering equity, systems change, consensus building, and strategic process through powerful networks of African American and Latinx leaders and allies, it is uniquely designed to redefine who is a philanthropist. Essentially, it embodies the principles of trust philanthropy. By reimagining the philanthropic sector; amplifying solutions by leaders of color; and utilizing the time, talent, and treasure of the collective, CoThinkk is yielding positive impact and ripples across its footprint.

CoThinkk continuously sets the stage to ask a set of ongoing critical questions regarding the power of permission: Who are you asking permission of? Why do you ask for permission? Does this situation necessitate waiting for permission? What will happen if you wait for permission? What will happen if you move forward without permission?

This nuanced and complicated dance is challenging for those who must take risks to amplify the voices of the unseen and unheard in service to change. Essentially, this notion of asking permission is like jumping double Dutch. If you're good at it, you are perfectly aware of the grade of the cement, the speed of the wind, and the height of the individuals turning the ropes. You're honest about your skill level. You sync with the rhythm of the ropes, the turners, and the sing-song rhyme to masterfully take a huge leap of faith, hoping to jump in at just the right moment and not end up on the ground, trying to detangle yourself from the ropes. As your skill improves, you begin to understand that permission, coupled with respect and trust, equals power.

The addition of power repositions permission as an invitation to a position of possibility and explicit choice. Adding power to permission anchors it deeply in a set of core beliefs that include collaboration, collective action, healing, trust, love, innovation, equity, and solidarity. The power of permission, then, honors you, the people, their assets, their capital, and their lived experiences in the very essence of community. When the intentional decision to surrender to the power of permission is made, traditional rules and requirements for permission are discarded and make way for new opportunities for inclusion, impact, and reimagining a new path forward. This type of beautiful surrender is the first step in the journey of purposeful alignment.

On my journey to purposeful alignment, this new perspective caused me to ask, "What could be possible if I fully anchored myself, my life, and all my work in the power of permission?" I decided to embrace a posture of accepting permission as a non-negotiable for having greater impact.

This work unveiled to me the following Permission Principles, which are critical to experiencing meaningful results:

- Permission Principle 1: Notice the Signals and the Signs, Then Assess

- Permission Principle 2: Say Yes

- Permission Principle 3: Embrace Positive Disruption and Activate Your Power

PERMISSION PRINCIPLE 1 :

NOTICE THE SIGNALS AND THE SIGNS, THEN ASSESS

I give myself permission to see things as they are, rather than create a false story about what I desire them to be.

As we began one of our long strategy meetings at work, we all piled into the boardroom and each hunkered down into our familiar spot. This was an important quarterly meeting, and we had invited all our partners together to discuss updates, new lessons, and strategy course corrections. Seated at the end of the long mahogany table, readying myself for the meeting, I felt as if I was having an out-of-body experience. Everyone seemed to speak and move in slow motion. The tension in the room was heavy, and I could tell I wasn't the only one who could sense it.

Nervousness filled every expression, whisper, and shared glance. The awkward body language seemed to carry a multitude of unspoken agendas. There were leaders at the table who I had known for years, strong souls who had always been intentional about their work. But here, they struggled to articulate ideas they had labored over in preparation for this big meeting. I could see the frustration, which seemed to stem from miscommunication. Highly capable people seemed challenged to move from theory to implementation. All this crescendoed in individuals speaking to one another in a way I had never experienced.

For people in our group, or new participants joining us, these dynamics might have appeared normal. But for me they were the culmination of multiple scenes I had witnessed play out over and over, leading to the acceptance of an important revelation. These were not normal dynamics, and no amount of denial would change that truth. I had tried to accept or ignore the drama playing out in front of me over weeks and months. I had whispered false stories to myself to justify the work and the effort of enduring these situations. After all, I was here in service to the community. I had to put up with this. But did I?

This wasn't the first time I witnessed this cultural dance. It had become all too familiar as it played out daily in the form of dominating language, disempowering thinking, and toxic behaviors that had become normalized. The critical components necessary to create just the right cultural gumbo—solidarity, mutual respect and caring, collaboration, curiosity, and consistent and authentic teamwork—were missing. What I was witnessing ran counter to everything I had been taught and learned over the course of my career. It was not enough for me to cover my mouth to avoid getting sick. Eventually, I would contract this virus that had infiltrated the entire organization, this disease, which I realized that day had been slowly eating away at my being and my desire to continue this work. That day marked the first inflection point of many. It was a signal that the Universe was not going to let me forget.

THE SIGNALS

They were all around me but
I was too buried in the work to see them.

Signals are a funny phenomenon. They show up in mysterious ways. Some appear as subtle reminders, coincidences, dreams, or incidents, blaring like a megaphone to jolt you and wake you up. Signals are ever present and can reveal themselves when you stop, sit still, watch, and listen. Being intentional about making space for yourself to just sit can be foreign to those who use the daily grind to meet obligations, check off the to-do list, and do what is required to make it through the day. Taking a moment to pause is often viewed as a luxury for many who do the heavy work to support community change efforts. You are torn between your calling to serve, and the need to balance the work with your personal life. This forces you to constantly weave the pieces together, like a rich tapestry, in an attempt to manage work-life integration.

Pausing and noticing is a critical first step that forces you to sit still and move into a discovery posture; a posture from which you can look at things more closely and get proximal. Proximity forces you to examine the interconnectedness of everything. It's not a big movement; it is a slight shifting to move you into a posture necessary to ask hard questions of yourself and of others. Proximity forces you to settle into the truth. This posture forces you to move from a place of implicitly speaking and expressing how you feel to an explicit place of noticing and settling into the facts. As a result, you give yourself permission to document and describe the things around you, the situations that play out over and over, and the conversations in a factual manner without raw emotion. Ultimately, the situation begins to reveal a colorful picture meant to do three things: 1) provide critical information; 2) provoke additional questions; and 3) serve as an important pulse check.

Pre-Retirement Space (margin annotation)

This discovery phase was one of the hardest for me to begin. I had to give myself permission to hold the possibility that it was okay for me to even embark on this journey. I needed to gather information about my environment, the relationships I had developed, and the work I was committed to doing. Never before had I taken a step-by-step approach to review these important aspects of my life at such depth. I questioned these newfound feelings and doubted I had the time, the space in my life, or the luxury to do this self-imposed self-exploration in the midst of moving important work. Even with these doubts, I knew I had to surrender to the audacity to ask hard questions of myself in order to move to a different place. I had entered a space where I was excited about the amazing work that would unfold.

In that space I realized I needed to give myself permission to ask the following questions. Consider exploring these questions for yourself:

- google Suit
- canvas (margin annotation)

1. What signals am I seeing? *I'm seeing A decline in my drive and passion. I'm a bit slower mental and physically. Technology Is not my passion*

2. What am I noticing about these signals? *Becoming louder and more profound*

3. How am I responding to these signals? *It's depressing, Challenging / hope/ It reveals that my responses are like waves. up then down*

4. What am I feeling and experiencing in my body, mind, and heart in response? *A bit Apprehensive about the unknown. my mind wonders about It the finianciances are Stable, as I feel like they are.*

5. What do I think this means? *Retirement - an Ending / begin. My body is tired of the 35 years of the Same routines. my heart is passionate about the classroom, The Co-workers. How will my heart handle the change of levels. Fight/ flight Forget/ Fold*

NOTICE AND ASSESS

I had to assess the signs and things I was noticing to determine what was true.

For most people, visiting the doctor's office is the last resort when you don't feel well, can't cure it yourself, and can't find the answer to your ailment via Dr. Google. When you finally arrive at the dreaded doctor's office, the nurse takes your vital signs—your temperature and your pulse. For me, this is one of the most nerve-racking parts of the appointment. I am more conscious of my breathing and my posture. All sorts of thoughts race through my mind: *Is something wrong? Does she hear something? Should I breathe slower? Why am I sweating?* All this thinking probably has an adverse effect on my vital signs. This experience is synonymous with how you might feel when you examine the signals that show up through experiences, interactions, language, and behaviors to alert you of trouble ahead.

As I checked the signals and documented what I was noticing at work, for the first time I silently explored what it would be like to trust what I felt. What if I said no to this space, to these people, and to this place? What would happen if I decided to reject that doing the work in this limited and transactional way was my only option?

Exploring these thoughts brought about a level of anxiety and a sense of possibility. Even the promise of knowing something better was possible, that I would welcome a new normal, wasn't enough to move me forward. I confided in close friends and colleagues, asking their opinions about how it would be perceived if I decided to do something else. What would be the backlash for my career, my finances, my reputation, and my work? I wrestled with these questions for weeks.

On a quiet Thursday evening, my phone rang. On the other end of the line was a friendly voice, a longtime mentor, friend, and colleague, well-respected in the sector, state, and region. As the conversation began, I could tell my friend knew something of the decision I had been struggling with. I needed an ally, but I didn't need someone to tell me what to do. This, I knew, was my decision alone.

"I'm team Tracey. So whatever you want to do, I'm supportive of it," came the encouraging words. "But I would only ask that you give it a couple more months. This is an important growth moment. We all have them."

I was glad to have such a supportive friend and colleague to logically guide my thinking through this difficult decision. The conversation put in motion a series of powerful questions and reflections and forced me to interrogate my state in a way I was not prepared to do. The moment was so uncomfortable for me that I felt nauseous, with cramping in the pit of my stomach. It was kind of like the inevitable bellyache that comes after eating greasy food. It tastes good to the tongue, but it doesn't agree with your stomach, and it leaves you with a weird aftertaste in your mouth and a sickness you can't reconcile. You can't quite throw up, but the feeling won't pass. (You know which emoji I am talking about.) I couldn't name this feeling. So I retreated to a thinking place. Quietly and suddenly, the feeling revealed itself. It was fear.

Fear can keep you paralyzed, in some instances, yet cause you to make commitments that don't serve you well in other situations. You get caught in a cycle of unspoken parameters and rules you unconsciously adopt as a part of what's "normal." This was so characteristic of my journey and my walk. In the face of these rules, I still was unwilling to see what was right in front of my fear. I believed if I reconciled these signals and interrogated them at the root, I would have to take some action. I would have to move, make a different decision, and set in motion a ripple I was not sure I was ready for.

In these situations, give yourself permission to ask:

1. What patterns are repeating themselves?

2. Who are the people involved? *My Family, Boss, Colleagues.*

3. What is the relationship between what I am seeing and what is being revealed?

4. What is the impact of this on me, my work, my role, the significance I seek to have in the world?

5. Is this really happening, or is all this my secret shadow(s) showing up?

As you explore your fears, give yourself permission to ask:

- What fears are stopping me from noticing and assessing? *Failure, Transition, Death, having no Schedule.*

- What could be the *best* outcome if I reconciled these signals with the truth? *I've worked 35 years for A nice Severence package and retirement benifits And I could live Comfortably*

- What's the *worst* that could happen if I reconciled the signals with the truth?

- What empowering thinking, feelings, and actions do I need to embrace?

- What disempowering thinking, feelings, and actions do I need to interrupt?

Scan QR code above for additional questions to explore and assess the signs and signals.

PERMISSION PRINCIPLE 2:

SAY YES

I had to interrupt the distance between the signals and my yes.

Interruption is an intentional action and serves as an important catalyst for introspection. This powerful tool is meant to disrupt the regular flow or sequence of events to facilitate powerful change or transition. Interruption shakes things up and allows what is unseen to rise to the top.

When you allow it to, interruption shines a light on the unseen and unspoken things. With that exposure, you can face what is true. You grant yourself permission to reconcile polarizing realities.

Interrupting the distance between your signals is a precursor for your yes. Interruption creates a space that causes disorientation because it forces you to examine all aspects of your life and the very foundation you have established to steady yourself throughout your work. By interrogating your values and priorities, you open the door for an awakening necessary for the old to disappear and the new to emerge.

GRAPPLE WITH WHAT SAYING YES COULD MEAN

The distance between your signals and your yes, represents a significant inflection point. Here, you are required to actively fill in the gap between your current state and what is possible for your life, your work, and your relationships. This critical exploration requires you to accept your current reality and to give yourself permission to just say yes. This frees

means to release your creative potential and take control of your reality, through peaceful actions, provocation or even agitation.
Michael Carthy.com.

you to shift your thinking, to ask hard questions, and to serve as a provocateur in scenarios where the heavy lifting is being done to create the perfect conditions to ensure the invisible is visible.

When you are ready to take this critical step forward, even without knowing what is next, you are saying yes to moving yourself from the fringes of your life to the center of it all. You are saying yes to healing and owning your own stuff, so you don't take it anywhere else or hinder future decision-making. You are saying yes to retooling and exploring. You are saying yes to creating ways to work differently and to have a greater impact. You are saying yes to thriving and being present in a new way.

Imagine a time when you said yes to something big and audacious. What allowed you to say yes?

Being more than a creative thinker.

Open the door for an awakening that is necessary for the old to disappear and the new to emerge.

We had been trying for months to get pregnant, I was nervous about the process and hopeful that, at the end, we would expand our family. IVF (in vitro fertilization) is a grueling process of doctor appointments, monitoring, exams, medicine, and countless shots. I hate going to the doctor. I hate shots even more. But I was willing to endure it all to keep my eyes on the prize—a healthy pregnancy and baby.

While I was facilitating a strategy brainstorming session with a cohort of colleagues, a call came in from my doctor's office. I could hardly contain my excitement as I excused myself from the meeting to take the call. The voice on the other end said, "Tracey, you're pregnant." A force of emotions welled up in my body, and I uttered the only response I could. "Really, are you sure?" Finally, after months of preparation and a successful embryo transfer procedure, we received the news we were waiting for. I immediately texted my husband the good news. We were both ecstatic.

It's funny, when you are pregnant, it's like you have a little secret no one knows except you. You walk around with a little smile that's missed by most. You don't even realize your face reveals the joy of what is growing inside of you. That's how I was for the first few weeks. And then, something strange occurred. My husband and I were on a casual walk, and I started bleeding. It was still pretty early in the pregnancy, so we decided to go the emergency room. The examination revealed all was well with the baby and with me, so we breathed a sigh of relief, chalked up the bleeding as normal, and went on with our lives. Throughout the following two weeks, the bleeding continued, on and off, but I kept going with my life and work.

On the cusp of a meeting I had spent weeks preparing for, my excitement level was high. It was the final session I needed to complete the budget recommendations for the work I was charged with. I wanted to ensure my rationale was grounded in data, informed by staff on the ground, and anticipated future opportunities being cultivated by the entire organization and by the sector. I was looking forward to so much. And then, it happened. I miscarried. I had never experienced a miscarriage of this type before. It was heartbreaking.

I sent a note to the leadership team, informing them I needed to take a couple of days off and explaining why. My two colleagues moved things forward in my absence. During this time, I should have grieved and leaned into my emotions and loss, but I didn't. I was too afraid to fully release all I was feeling—the dreams, the hope, the excitement about bringing another new life into our family—out of fear that I would not be able to show up at work, ready and confident to continue in my role.

When I returned to work, I was met with support from my team, but I was extremely fatigued and still processing my emotions throughout the day. The first of two budget meetings had been scheduled the week I returned, so I needed time to digest the information from the meeting I missed in order to prepare. I arrived at the meeting with most of the budget recommendations complete, but not all.

I was soon met with the reality that I was expected to have all the final pieces complete, even in the face of my recent situation. On top of that, I was using a new collaborative process to create transparency and alignment by connecting all the foundation's capital—social, moral, intellectual, relational, and financial—with an explicit approach that tracked with a forecasted budget to support strategic implementation. It was a lot. In this moment, I should have paused and paid attention to the signals, but I didn't. I continued and worked tirelessly over the next several days to ensure I could submit the final budget recommendations.

If I had interrogated that moment using a lens of truth, I would have been able to say, "You are not being kind to yourself, Tracey. You should be more explicit about what you need and what is realistic in the face of this expectation. You need more time off." Rushing back to work and pretending like I was all right did not serve me well and sent the wrong message about how I valued myself. My actions set in place a norm for how others would value me as well. I had to interrupt the distance between the signals and my yes, and this was the beginning.

Imagine a critical scenario in your life when you missed the opportunity to care for yourself, a time that might have offered the opportunity to grapple with what saying yes could mean.

- What happened in your situation?

- How did you react?

- How did you care for yourself?

- How did others care for you?

- How did they not care for you?

- What was your role and responsibility in this situation?

NAVIGATE UNFAMILIAR TERRITORY

I had to be willing to embrace disorientation
in service to a larger purpose.

Navigating unfamiliar territory is probably some of the hardest work to do. As I drove home from the office, I couldn't help but reflect on the week. A week filled with internal strategy meetings, learning from amazing community leaders, and realizing a hard truth. I had to be honest with myself about the amount of effort and energy I was expending to reach the strategic goals of the initiatives I was leading. All this work was happening while I navigated an unspoken backdrop filled with tension between a desire for transformational change and a desire for transactional change, a resistance to change and process, and navigating countless micro aggressions.

As I took the onramp to the main highway and found myself in the flow of traffic with cars of all shades and sizes moving at racecar speeds, I realized I had done this drive so many times that it had become all too familiar. I noted how I switched lanes in anticipation of the change in the grade of the highway when it shifted suddenly because it hadn't been repaired yet. I noted the exit that contained the only gas station for miles, bustling with cars as drivers tried to frantically get on the outermost shoulder of the highway to avoid causing an accident. I saw the sign for the boutique winery I passed every day, which seemed to have an endless number of cars packed into its small parking lot. I knew this route like the back of my hand. The reality of this all too familiar scene caused me to think deeply about what would compel me to lean in and navigate unfamiliar territories and paths moving forward.

Pathways are endless trails defined by a multitude of twists and turns that are hard to predict. Sometimes, there are blind spots that create disorientation and force you to trust your instincts in a new way to ensure you can continue successfully. Just when you think you've discovered the patterns of the pathway, it shifts suddenly, forcing you to recalibrate and revisit your strategy. Uncertainty enters, bringing a level of frustration, fear, and trepidation. In a fleeting moment, just as you are about to turn back and give up, the next corner reveals something amazing that you were not expecting.

Navigating unfamiliar territory is a part of the journey to purposeful alignment and can take the form of new thinking, ideas, and self-reflections—both good and bad—as well as adjusting the lens with which you see the world. Newness along this pathway allows you to work a new muscle that necessitates a paradigm shift that creates readiness to confront the reality of your current state, situation, and posture. This is the work required to interrupt the space of what is real and true in your life, in your work, and in your relationships, in order to say yes. The interruption begs for a new way of thinking and of showing up in this work.

The first step to move into a yes position is often painful and full of self-doubt. The precursor is meant to jolt you and compel you forward to a state of disorientation. The process of saying yes can place you in unfamiliar territory. The interesting thing about navigating a new space is that it forces you to be aware, to steady yourself, and to adapt in a moment's time to a shifting context shaped by your thoughts, your actions, and your feelings. This requires you to lean in to your circle of influence, to begin a faith walk, and to embrace discomfort and ambiguity.

As you move into a yes position, give yourself permission to ask:

1. What past or current moments of courage will I have to draw upon to face the fears I will encounter when interrupting my familiar pathway?

2. What ambiguity and discomfort might I have to face, and what unexpected surprises might that present?

3. Who in my community will guide, support, and celebrate me on this journey?

4. What new boundaries will I have to be explicit about to imagine what my yes will look like?

5. What is the new narrative I can imagine by saying yes?

Scan QR code above for additional questions to help you navigate unfamiliar territory.

PERMISSION PRINCIPLE 3 :

EMBRACE POSITIVE DISRUPTION AND ACTIVATE YOUR POWER

Nothing happens without action and movement.

In 2013, TEDx created an event focused on the theme "Positive Disruption." The website described it in the following manner: "Disruption is usually unwelcome. It represents conflict, chaos, and potential danger. We discourage disruptive behavior in our homes and our societies, often favoring passivity and compliance instead. But disruption can be a positive—sometimes vital—catalyst for change. It can challenge old assumptions, ignite conversations, activate authorities, and expose new possibilities. Disruption can shed a unique light on difficult issues, giving a fresh, urgent perspective to the challenges of our global community."

Positive disruption enables the activation of power, allowing old narratives to be challenged and making way for the activation of what's possible. My relationship and journey with power has always been complicated. I have constantly had to adjust my proximity to it as an agent for change. Power is a concept that has fueled many conflicting feelings. On one end of the spectrum, as an ally, it has served as a source of personal growth, allowed me to support others, and served as a tool to spark change. In these instances, I learned to embrace power, whether my own or power derived from standing on the shoulders and legacy of leaders who came before me. Meanwhile, activating power in its most traditional definition has left many tender spots, hurtful memories, and

30

uncomfortable references to moments that caused harm or trauma in my life.

When I reflect on the concept of activating power, I wrestle with the negative image conjured up. I see individuals and leaders focused on exerting power in the form of control, influence, or imposing limitations on others, as opposed to sharing and building power. I see images of more traditional hierarchies, which have either have been named or appointed by others as powerful. In these scenarios, those in power lead or direct in an oppressive, abusive, extractive, and exploitative manner. Theirs is the type of power that expects all others to voluntarily concede power to them.

Those who do so temper their unspoken fear in order to feed the leader's need for control. Similarly, the type of power fueled by intimidation and abuse creates a culture of toxicity. In this environment, opposing opinions are met with punitive repercussions reinforced by others who have learned to navigate and normalize the actions of those in power. That is the old-world view of power. It is outdated and antiquated and calls for a new relationship that moves away from the old to evolve into something new.

Ideal activation of power is very much about the activation of self. It is the intentional action of each individual to transform self and community to facilitate positive impact in every aspect of life. This intentional action is not about holding power over others. Instead, it is about anchoring squarely in the values of collaboration, collective impact, seeding, nurturing, trust, and love. By anchoring the activation of power in these key values, the collective challenges the very idea of power and activates itself to wield power from a place of sharing. This allows for the collaborative building of power with others to facilitate significant transformation leading to sustainable change.

Change and transformation do not happen without action and movement. In order to move, you have to feel comfortable owning your own power and intentionally choosing a different path forward. A path that has the possibility of changing the trajectory of your work, your relationships, and your life in a way much more aligned with the role you are called to serve in this world. Yet, even in the face of owning your power, you must shift your thinking, your feelings, and your actions.

By leaning in to the truth about the signals you see, you notice the patterns and begin the process of shifting your thinking. When you shift your thinking, you can drop down into your feelings, while exploring and reimagining what saying yes could reveal. Finally, you reach the point of activating your power, where you own your voice and your vote. This is the space of taking ownership of the future trajectory of your journey. This ownership is active and forward-thinking. It is the explicit and intentional decision to wield your power in a way that positions you in a manner aligned with your purpose, your leadership, and your role in this ecosystem for change. It begins with you having the courage to take the first step.

Give yourself permission to ask:

1. What positive disruptions do I need to identify or cause to activate my power

2. What permissions do I need to give myself regarding this power?

3. What does it mean to activate my power?

4. What past or current courage will I draw upon to face the fears holding me back from leaning in to and activating my power?

5. What guidance, support, and celebration will I need from my community in this moment?

Scan QR code above for additional questions to explore positive disruption and activation.

THE INFLECTION POINT

I wasn't willing to concede my power; therefore, I had to go.

I had arrived at the office two hours early to prepare for meetings. I was excited that we were at the right inflection point, where things would begin to move very fast. I wanted to check in with leadership to ensure I was tracking with the broader conversation and aligning with decisions that were being moved forward. While I was in my office, assessing the huge whiteboard colored with projects, ideas, names, and deadlines, my cell phone rang. As we began our normal check-in, the voice on the line said, "Can we have a real conversation?" *I was under the impression all our conversations were real.* Obviously, this one would be different.

"You are not doing your job," the voice said, following my silence.

I was stunned, speechless. After a long pause, I finally found my voice. "What exactly do you mean? Give me an example of ways I'm not performing the work to your satisfaction?" I was poised for a barrage of one-liners, but there were none. Not one shred of evidence was provided to support the accusation that I was failing in my duties.

I slowly leaned back into my chair. In that moment, I knew this wasn't about me. It was about something deeper, a fundamental misalignment of ideals regarding true transformational change and what it takes to facilitate it. It was about fear and disorientation. I knew the situation would have engulfed me totally without this clarity, and I understood that if I yielded to this false and shaky narrative about my work, I would become complicit in practices that were counter to my values, lived experiences, and training. It was time for me to pivot.

You have the permission and the
responsibility to take action.

This was my full-circle moment. Thankfully, these moments don't come often. But when they come, I have to pay attention. I took stock of all the signals and all the assessing I had been doing for months. I knew I was not purposefully aligned. I was in the wrong place doing the right work. I needed to say yes to reimagining what a new normal could look like for me. I owed it to myself and to my elders, who had seeded so much time, energy, and knowledge into me. This moment was calling me, along with other change agents, into something bigger. I could no longer stay in places and relationships were content to do surface-level work or who caused trauma and toxicity.

These moments of clarity do not have to be fueled by something traumatic or even monumental. The process of taking back your power begins with a settling within yourself that you have the permission and the responsibility to act. This is a necessary precursor to this transformational process of surrendering. You have to surrender to the facts, surrender to your burning desire to be purposefully aligned, and surrender to not knowing what is next. Just be open to possibilities.

This type of surrendering is unfamiliar territory. It was disorienting for me. I was used to moving things. The words "catalyst," "weaver," and "change guru" were fixed into my vocabulary. I was forcing myself to own my power and act in a different way. It wasn't action for a cause or for family or friends; it was action for me and leaning in to possibility. If I moved to action in this very moment, I could seed something amazing and transformational. By taking a leap on this faith walk, I could level up my leadership and impact. I could renegotiate how I do my work. Finally, I could be both impactful and unapologetically happy, and I could thrive. I was saying I was going to lean in to a transformational process that would enable purposeful alignment.

Give yourself permission to ask:

1. What roles do I need to let go of in order to give myself permission to act?

2. What choices will I have to make personally and relationally to have positive impact?

3. What little actions and big actions am I prepared to take?

4. What past or current courage will I draw upon to face the fears I am grappling with?

5. Who do I need in my community to guide, support, and celebrate me in this moment?

THE TURNING POINT

The voice in my head kept saying, "Not yet."
The voice in my heart said, "It's time."

I finally got it. I took the first step into the shift. I fully opened myself up to the transformation process, but I needed a final push. I was sitting in a meeting at work when the caller ID revealed a number from a friend who rarely called me. I couldn't answer at the time, so shortly thereafter, a notification of a voice message showed up. My gut said it must be urgent. Instead of checking the message, I immediately called back. As I stepped out of the meeting, the person who answered the phone said, "Kelly has passed away." I felt a sudden sharpness in the center of my chest as I steadied myself against the wall outside of the board room. *Breathe, Tracey. Breathe.* I had to finish the last leg of the agenda.

Kelly, a dear colleague and friend, was the third person in my life who had been diagnosed with cancer within in a three-year period and the second to pass away. I'd experienced this type of loss before in my life, with the death of my first son Ayden, who was stillborn. I recognized this as a pivotal moment when things get very clear really fast.

In that moment, I knew six things:

1. I needed to take a courageous leap of faith to say yes to me. I had been moving a million miles a minute. I had sacrificed self-care in service to doing important work. This call could have been about me.
2. I desired to fully align my gifts, talents, values, approach, and heart.
3. I had to be a game changer and support others in amplifying their superpowers.

4. My work would explicitly sit at the intersection of community economic development, education, health and wellbeing, and leadership development.

5. I could freely advance the efforts of CoThinkk and other social change philanthropy models as a way to reimagine the field of philanthropy.

6. I had to say yes to supporting systems change from a different vantage point. I had to say yes to experimenting and retooling to have greater and deeper impact to solve some of the most vexing issues facing our country.

The Universe had sent a powerful signal that something had to change within me. I couldn't play it safe. The change had to start with my ability to activate myself and put things in motion to be purposefully aligned. I had finally agreed to interrupt the voice in my head that was saying, "Not yet," and surrender to moving forward and taking action.

The concept of surrendering is about letting go. It is about being in agreement with yourself to take a new walk of faith into the unknown. At the same time, surrendering provides a level of freedom and the possibility for setting new boundaries within yourself, with others, and with everything around you. Surrender leads to a type of freedom that requires you to just sit still and wait; to believe deeply, in every ounce of who you are, that everything will be okay; to take it further and know your entire life will be an amazing adventure that has yet to be imagined and can be whatever you dream into existence.

Give yourself permission to ask:

1. What voices and narratives do I need to interrupt in order to surrender to what is possible?

2. What final push or words of encouragement do I need from my community to move forward?

3. What fears do I need to confront in this moment?

THE PIVOT

You cannot carry this into next year. There is much work to be done. This chapter has to end to make room for a new beginning.

The ability to shift your posture and lean in to your power, particularly if you are not used to doing it for yourself, can be unsettling. You move from disempowering thinking to powerful thinking. You surrender to doing the hard work to pivot and lean in to that space.

I often talked on the phone during my morning commute. There was always someone I needed to check in with and doing so during the hour-long drive allowed for quiet space and uninterrupted time. One morning, in my commute conversation, my close friend Katrina said, "You can't carry this forward into next year. You have to move today." What she was saying was true. I had stayed too long, and I had to say no to this chapter so I could make room for new dreams, visions, work, adventures, relationships, and possibilities.

If I hung on to this space out of fear, comfort, or obligation, I would be acting in disobedience to the new space I was being called into. This new space required my full attention. If I looked back, I could be disoriented and distracted, and my lens would get cloudy. The glance back would prevent me from seeing the opportunities presenting themselves right in front of me. I needed to unapologetically create what was to come for me. I had to interrupt my thinking. I had to innovate and reconcile my feelings, get uncomfortable, push past the fear, and release the obligation I had made. I had to amplify my actions.

I had to first shift my *thinking* from disempowering to powerful thinking. I had to face the narrative I was telling myself and allowing others to tell about me. I had to be willing to take the mystique out of this moment. I needed to stop sparring with myself and drop down totally into this new possibility. I had to embrace my positional power and renegotiate existing relationships. I had to set new boundaries. I had to get proximal to what had been and move into what had to be. I had to inventory the tools in my toolkit, which I had been collecting and fine tuning, and use them for purposeful alignment.

Secondly, I had to shift my *feelings* from disempowering to powerful feelings. I had to shift from *thinking* questions and reflections to *feeling* questions. I had to assess and mind the tender spots, the biases, and the assumptions I had held for so long. I had to cope with my feelings in order to be in new, trusting relationships. I had to define for myself what it looks like and how it feels to cover someone differently. I had to know, unquestionably, how I would consciously manage my feelings in uncomfortable and new places.

Lastly, I had to shift my *actions and behaviors* from disempowering to powerful. I had to shift my language. I had to consciously and intentionally do my own work in areas that were foreign for me. I had to be willing to say, describe, and interrogate the things I had allowed to linger for the past ten years. I examined complicity at new levels and stopped editing myself in order to unleash undeniable creativity and unique perspectives from an elevated posture.

This was the beginning of bringing my full self into every aspect of my life, the beginning of my new future. And I was ready.

* * *

As I walked to the podium at the Institute for Emerging Issues Conference, which was themed "Innovation in Civic Engagement," and looked over the packed hotel ballroom in my hometown of Asheville, North Carolina, I saw so many familiar faces. The topic felt so natural to me. I knew it like a fish knows water. I felt honored when asked to introduce the segment, talk about the innovative philanthropic work I'd been leading in partnership with community leaders, and introduce a panel of regional pioneers catalyzing new models and creating tremendous impact.

This speech marked the beginning of my year-long journey of moving purposeful alignment from the fringes of my life to the center.

By centering this important work as a critical non-negotiable in my life, I was activating a series of yeses and creating clear boundaries with my nos regarding anything that caused disorientation and distraction. With this new version of myself, I sent a strong signal to others that this moment was calling us all to be bigger than ourselves. I was demonstrating that, collectively, we needed to move from a posture of permission to leaning in to transformation to impact complex social change.

To do this effectively, I knew three important things:

1. I had to practice this process myself.
2. In order to practice, I had to stop and create space.
3. I had to seek respite and healing.

As you lean in to transformation, give yourself permission to ask:

1. What thinking, narratives, assumptions, and biases do I need to shift in order to have greater impact and seek purposeful alignment?

2. What tender spots do I need to address?

3. What questions do I have to grapple with?

4. What type of solidarity do I need from my circle of influence at this important inflection point?

5. What permissions, actions, and behaviors am I compelled to amplify, interrupt, or innovate in service to purposeful alignment?

Scan the QR code above for additional questions to explore positive disruption and activation.

THE YES MAP

Let's dream out loud together and begin to imagine what your first yes would be as you give yourself permission. Please use the diagram below to identify your first yes. Then, imagine what you think your three nos would need to be to support your first yes.

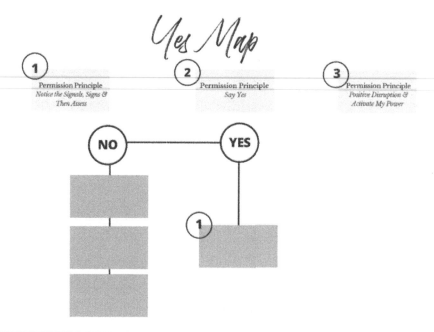

1 — Permission Principle
Notice the Signals, Signs & Then Assess

2 — Permission Principle
Say Yes

3 — Permission Principle
Positive Disruption & Activate My Power

Choosing Purposeful Alignment
The Messy Middle of Transformation

CHOICE 2:

LEAN IN TO TRANSFORMATION

Let go of what is no longer serving you,
as in the lyrics from "Bag Lady,"
by Erykah Badu.

TRANSFORMATION TRAUMA

Transformation doesn't have to be traumatic; it can be restorative.

My husband, Edmund, and I had been grappling with it for weeks; this nagging question about the nature of change and the sharp emotions it evokes in everyone. As we sat in the office together, he at the desk, reading through his assignment for his master's program in cybersecurity, and me on the soft carpet in front of his desk, we entered one of our well-established "kitchen talks."

For us, kitchen talks are those intimate conversations at the end of a long week, during which we discuss situations or issues we've encountered and things we've learned about ourselves. This time, our conversation was particularly ripe. I could not stop talking about how the complexity of systems-level impact necessitates change. Theoretically, it makes sense that making change at the level required for transformation creates discomfort. Change may seem daunting, but when it is upon you, you experience a range of emotions. You either lean in and embrace it, or you resist, challenge, or stop it.

Edmund could not stop talking about the complexity of technology and how the competitive global marketplace necessitates disruption. As users of technology in so many areas of our lives, we understand the necessity of change in that area. Again, we either lean in and embrace it, or we resist, challenge, or stop it. How could two individuals, working in two vastly different sectors, arrive at the same conclusion? How could change evoke similar challenges and opportunities in the social sector and in the field of technology? The answers were buried deep in a case study he was reading for his class assignment. The author called this dilemma "transformation trauma."

Transformation trauma refers to significant and rapid change introduced within an organization or a complex issue that significantly disrupts, affects, and reorganizes long-standing practices with the goal of greater innovation or deeper impact (Munro and Khan, 2013). This sparked a more intense conversation that continued into the next morning as we prepared for the day. As I brushed my teeth and he put in his contact lenses, we discussed those powerful words—transformation trauma. It felt like such an oxymoron.

Transformation is a thorough or dramatic change in form, or an act, process, or instance of transforming. When I examine the definition of transformation, I perceive it as good and positive, something everyone should want or desire. In many beloved self-help books of this generation, we see references such as transform your life, education for self-transformation, digital transformation, challenge and transformation, and the list goes on. Transformation is presented as revolutionary, elevating, and readying one for the next level of something magnificent.

Trauma, on the other hand, is a behavioral state resulting from severe mental or emotional stress. Most often, people view trauma as scary, something intended to cause harm or injury that should be feared and avoided at all cost. If this is how we see change in the context of solving the world's complex challenges, it's no wonder we have such a sharp range of responses to embrace, resist, challenge, or stop it. How can we create enough healthy tension to embrace transformation and change without it being traumatic? How can we unpack this phenomenon in a way that addresses deeply entrenched social issues that will impact generations to come?

If I was going to lean in to transformational change that could propel me forward with a clear line of sight, I would first have to name what I was feeling and experiencing. This transformation would have to be strategically positioned in a way that was uncomfortable, but not traumatic. Therefore, I had to figure out how to create the necessary safe space to acknowledge and process my feelings without judgment. I had to allow myself to contend with how change would impact me, my work, and my relationships. After all, this was a new space and I had to build in flexibility. I had to be honest about preset timelines, expectations, and goals throughout the change process. I had to create a vision of purposeful alignment grounded in the elements of the emergent practice of "test, do, and learn." Giving myself space and permission to adjust the pathway to get there, I knew I would have to do a retrospective review, to interrogate past and current narratives to craft an evolved vision for the future.

My process involved examining and aligning existing and untapped skills, talents, and resources needed to amplify my vision for the future. I had to honestly explore questions about the accuracy of the picture I had painted. Had I done a good job in doing this work? Had I been playing the right role up to this point? Had my role been helpful or harmful? Which practices had I created that were healthy and positive, and which were not? I had to get intimately familiar and comfortable with change. I had to adopt new practices for identifying when fear of the unknown sneaks in and for determining how to address it. I had to learn to identify blind spots, ongoing concerns, and insecurities. At the same time, I stepped into the work of creating some clarity, a little bit of anchoring, and critical experimentation in this space of transformation. Finally, I had to face a fundamental question, one that constantly haunts me and would be ever present on this journey: How can I embrace transformation without sparring with it and without it being traumatic for me?

Integrating these new practices on the journey of transformation can propel you forward and help eliminate the trauma of change. To guide you on your journey, there are four Transformation Principles to support you:

- Transformation Principle 1: Reposition Your Stance

- Transformation Principle 2: Embrace Respite and Healing

- Transformation Principle 3: Center Yourself

- Transformation Principle 4: Retool and Experiment

TRANSFORMATION PRINCIPLE 1:

REPOSITION YOUR STANCE

I was tired. Rather than sit in that reality, I kept moving until I couldn't move anymore. My stance was slumped and leaning to the side, and I had a slight wobble in my gait.

During a leadership program developed by CoThinkk in 2017, in Asheville, I was introduced to the principles of movement work by Erin Byrd. In her session, she talked about four elements required to facilitate lasting change and impact for movements tackling complex issues. These elements, from Forward Stance, an integral practice developed by Norma Wong in collaboration with Forward Together, consist of stance, energy, rhythm, and awareness.

The introduction of these four simple elements set in motion an introspective process, which felt like a tsunami, during an exercise. I was paired with Erin, in a very intimate conversation, to interrogate the positioning of transformational impact within and outside of systems. The deep questioning and dialogue continued right up to the last second of the bell ringing to alert each team to pause and come back to the full group. The conversation left a lingering of chatter in my head that I could not shake. A level of awakening was created in me that was not going away and would follow me through this transformational process.

The juxtaposition of these simple elements was catalytic, compelling me to examine my role, my impact, and my voice from various positions within an ecosystem of change. The lingering questions led to unwavering questioning about what would be possible if I no longer worked within the system. What would be possible if I shifted the way I worked within the system? What would be possible if I worked on the fringes of the systems I desired to shift? What if I worked totally outside of the system in this innovative space? What would be possible if I explored a combination of these options?

ELEMENTS TO FACILITATE LASTING CHANGE

Exploring these elements more deeply creates space to explore what is possible and provides an easy access point to begin the deep conversation regarding transformation.

STANCE

The power of transformation requires the energy, the will, the drive, and the stance to move you forward. Stance is your physical orientation to the world. More specifically, it positions you to be clear about what you want to do and what is standing in your way. During transformational change, your stance must be forward facing and directionally balanced. According to Byrd, "Many progressive movements have a defensive stance that emphasizes protection, pushing back, and preventing things from happening, holding aground, and a culture of no."

Forward stance, on the other hand, promotes shifting to the offensive, and moving to a position of core strength. Interestingly, in my everyday work I am committed to change, to forward motion, to using my core strengths. I embrace the ambiguity of systems work and structure, but in my everyday life I'm pretty predictable. I can be caught ordering the same meal at every restaurant—Caesar salad with blackened salmon and a glass of water. I can't help but chuckle at the juxtaposition of these two sides of my personality. Many people grapple with this same issue. It may look different in each of us, but there is a natural internal sparring that happens on the journey to change.

ENERGY

Energy, another essential element of Norma Wong's principles of movement work, has two powerful sides that both propel and attract. In its most powerful form, in guiding purposeful alignment, energy can spur people to support a cause, rise above challenges, and become active participants rather than passive bystanders. The concept that like attracts like is true for both positive and negative energy. When your energy is negative, you are drawn to situations, relationships, and issues that reflect where you are in that moment. Conversely, when your energy is positive, you are aligned with opportunities that match your thriving, dynamic energy.

RHYTHM

Part of forward stance is recognizing the rhythms within and around you to maintain a sustainable pace. According to Byrd and Wong, a sustainable rhythm recognizes the different paces, builds in phases, and intentionally manages restorative pauses. When rhythm is too fast, too slow, erratic, or does not pause, your stance will shift out of balance. When you are in sync with your rhythm, you are able to create a deep awareness that enables you to pause. This allows you to yield to the temptation to push on beyond your limits, while creating the optimal environment to sustain momentum.

AWARENESS

As Erin wrapped up her talk, she focused on the concept of awareness as the perception of what is happening around you. It is ideally broad and as objective as possible, forcing you to see, think, and process your understanding. With a keen sensibility, you can gain more awareness by being connected to your body and understanding the perceptions of others. Although, awareness was the last point Byrd made in the presentation, I was struck by how it is probably one of the most important points. Without an acute awareness, it is hard to adjust your stance, to balance your energy, or even be aware of your rhythm. If you are not actively connected to your body, how can you know what your natural rhythm is and know where to adjust?

✳ ✳ ✳

I'm an early riser. And when I say early, I mean I'm sometimes awake at 3:00 a.m. For a long time in my career, I wore this like a badge of honor. It was not odd for those who knew me well to say, "I was not surprised to get your email that early, Tracey." One former colleague was traveling in the wee hours of the morning and called me out of the blue because he was having a hard time staying up and needed someone to talk to. I answered the phone, fully awake, and he laughed. "I knew you would be up and could help carry me to the finish line on this long drive," he said.

I didn't know any better. This had become my normal. I truly believed this was my rhythm, how I best used my energy. This "awake before dawn" persona was my posture because I did not have awareness. But that all changed the day I pushed too hard. I had worked twelve-hour days for nearly a week, and I was on a roll. My body was giving me indications that I was going beyond my limit, but I didn't listen. By the end of day six, my stomach hurt, my head hurt, and my body throbbed in a way I had never felt before. I had pushed myself too far. This space was new to me. This was my moment of awareness. My body and mind were telling me it was time for rest. The physical warnings were indisputable—rest or suffer the consequences. The mental indicators were less obvious, but apparent, nonetheless.

As soon as I closed the door to my house, all I could do was lie down in my bed. I figured a short nap would refresh me enough to handle some tasks around the house before picking up my laptop to clear up a few lingering items I felt I needed to complete before I began to truly rest. The rest was necessary and welcomed, and my sleep came quickly.

After what I thought might have been an hour or two, I awoke to a little person's warm body pressed firmly against mine, making a letter C. He tried to get as close as he could to snuggle, as if to imprint his little body on mine. I could smell his hair, and I saw his little hand on my leg.

Suddenly, he sensed that I was awake, and he turned to look at me, eye to eye. "Are you okay, Mama?" The sweetness of his voice was like a melody, one I had missed hearing for much too long.

"Yes, baby. I'm awake. What are you doing here in bed with me?"

"I was so worried about you," he said. "You usually don't sleep like this."

Immediately, my eyes searched the room for my phone so I could check the time. The white digital numbers read 2:57. The sunlight beamed through the room, so I knew it must be afternoon and not the still of the early morning. All I could remember was climbing into bed at 7:00 the night before. My memory didn't register awakening at all in the hours between—not to go to the bathroom, not to greet my husband, not to eat, not even to check on my baby. I had slept for twenty hours straight. Yet, I was still tired.

In that moment I looked into my baby's eyes and knew this new awareness had to bring a shift. It was screaming at the top of its lungs that I was not being kind to myself. I had been neglecting my mind, body, and spirt. This new awareness called out in such a powerful way that I understood I couldn't adjust my stance, choose my rhythm, or align my energy if I didn't find respite. "It's times to rest," I said to myself.

Energy, rhythm, and awareness all impact your stance. All three have to work in tandem as you reposition yourself to be purposefully aligned. So many precursors must be in place to ready and steady you in your stance. My journey had to begin with restoration through seeking respite, resting and healing, and then moving to center myself. Lastly, I had to decide to reimagine my future—or, at least my next move.

THE BEGINNING

Every journey has a beginning. My journey of respite began with two beautiful gifts. The first came in the form of peace of mind regarding our family finances. Our months of planning and discussions provided the reassurance that we would be financially secure until I was ready to make my next move. The second gift came from a friend and colleague. Her email arrived at the end of an especially tiring day. For a moment, I considered putting off reading it until the next day. But I clicked on her name and read: *We need to send someone to Italy for the Aspen Institute Leadership Globalization and the Quest for Common Values Seminar. We would like to extend the invitation to you, Tracey. We need your answer right away because the Symposium is in two and half weeks.*

I was in disbelief. I had never been to Italy. My reply was polite. "Thank you, but I can't possibly go." How could I, knowing our finances would take a hit from an unplanned trip? Not only that, was it fair to leave all the childcare responsibilities to my husband, particularly given his strenuous travel schedule? Seconds after I hit "send," my phone rang.

"Tracey, you have nothing else to do. Every good sabbatical requires a trip somewhere new to jumpstart things. You are the perfect person to go."

I declined again, while demonstrating lots of appreciation. Her final words rung in my ears as I hung up, "It's here if you want it. You just have to say yes. It's paid for."

I sat there, holding the phone and surprised at how quickly and easily I had arrived at the conclusion that this trip wasn't for me. I had decided to decline this generous offer. Whether out of respect for our budget, concern for how things would get done in my absence, or feeling gluttonous, particularly given the amazing gift I had already received, I wasn't sure. But saying no felt wrong, as if I was denying myself the very gift I had been seeking.

"Why can't I go? Who said I can't go?" I asked in a soft voice, speaking to no one but myself. "My family will be okay for five days. It's okay to accept this gift to be with other leaders from across the globe, tackling complex change, challenging assumptions, and thinking together about a better world. This is what purposeful alignment looks like." I had to embrace this moment and yield to what was happening. It was the right time in my life for this level of awareness. I needed this. I emailed back and said yes, then breathed a sigh of relief. It was a baby step in the direction of my next level of awareness.

When faced with the opportunity to reposition your stance, allow yourself to ask and answer these critical questions:

1. What empowering actions am I prepared to take to reposition my stance?

2. What empowering thinking and feelings do I need to manifest?

3. What or who from my circle of influence do I need to help me lean in to this space?

4. What disempowering thinking is standing in the way of my awareness?

5. What disempowering feelings are standing in the way of my rhythm and energy?

7.

Scan QR code above for additional questions to help reposition your stance.

TRANSFORMATION PRINCIPLE 2:

EMBRACE RESPITE AND HEALING

I slept for forty-five days. I was tired. My energy was not attracting or propelling; it was static and flat.

As I lay flat on my back, I shifted my pillow to look out the window adjacent to our bed to see a beautiful sunrise. It emerged like a phoenix rising from the treetops. Branches, still bare from the winter frost, seemed to stretch upward in a desperate request of the beautiful orange glow that ushered in the new day. I could not remember the last time I had watched the sunrise. It had been years since I was able to remain in my bed long enough to watch the sunlight show through the morning hours. In response to the beautiful scene, I smiled and then drifted back to sleep.

RESPITE

Suddenly, I heard a shifting in the corner of the room. It was my husband.

"Are you okay?" he asked with concern in his voice. "I've never seen you sleep this late and this much. I don't think I've ever seen you take a nap in the middle of the day. I just want to make sure you're okay."

I took a moment to orient myself, as he adjusted his laptop. He had relocated his entire office to our bedroom, while I was asleep, so he could watch over me. Indeed, he was worried about me. As I sat up in bed, I rubbed my tired eyes and stretched slowly, feeling slight muscle aches in my back and limbs. "I've been sleeping so much, but I'm still so tired," I said.

"If you're tired you should give yourself permission to go back to sleep," he said, matter-of-factly.

He made it sound so simple, as if there was nothing else to do but sleep. I wished that were true, but my mind tried to remind me of all the other things I should be doing. Admitting I was tired was so hard. I was brought up to keep it moving. How dare I say I was tired when others are working so hard around me? I realized, in that moment, that I could not participate in a transformational process if I was tired. My body would not respond, and this moment of respite, although foreign, was such an amazing gift.

Discomfort is an important part of transformation. It's a powerful feeling and experience that you either resist, embrace, or challenge. In this process, I realized discomfort was a new friend, walking alongside me on this journey. I had to build a new relationship with discomfort, as well as with the requirement to rest and heal. I stopped apologizing for the need to go to bed early. I started connecting with people online rather than driving to meetings. I created new rituals, like taking a bath each morning and using essential oils. The frantic morning routine with my son transitioned to laughter and moving slowly. I began sitting on the front porch and saying no to creating tasks and activities that distracted me and no longer served me. As a result, I began to enjoy my days more. I carved out more time for me and reserved less time for those outside of my inner circle.

At first, I had to rehearse what I would say to others about not being available. My CoThinkk family stepped in, and four core members took on the responsibility of answering emails to free me from this daily task. Finally, I said it. "I'm on sabbatical, and I have to rest." Whew! That was hard. Even in the midst of learning to say no, I still felt the responsibility to be available for my team.

I had asked my husband to drive me to a meeting I was committed to attending. This was the last meeting external to CoThinkk I would appear at for a while. As I greeted everyone prior to the meeting, a young lady approached me and said, "I'm surprised to see you here." She looked me up and down. Based upon her tone and body language, it was obvious she didn't want me there. Two weeks earlier, I would have explained and apologized. Yet, with this newfound freedom and the energy charged within from weeks of much-needed rest, I simply said, "That's funny. I've missed seeing you too." I sat in that moment and realized I had met my commitment to attend and support the important work being led at the meeting. That brief encounter served as an important reminder that I needed to pay attention and honor this journey and how I was using my energy.

Within an hour, I was exhausted, and needed to excuse myself from the remainder of the meeting. My husband had been waiting in the car for me. As we drove back home, I realized this pause and choosing to leave the meeting to take care of myself without apology were huge confirmation that I was doing the right work for me to be purposefully aligned, to be impactful. I had more work to do. My work started with asking and answering some deep, revealing questions.

As you lean in to healing and respite, give yourself permission to ask:

1. What disempowering thinking do I need to shift?

2. What disempowering feelings do I need to shift?

3. What disempowering actions do I need to shift?

4. What narratives and fears do I need to interrupt to rest so I can have the space to be purposefully aligned?

5. Where do I need to use my energy?

6. What do I need from my circle of influence in order to find respite and to implement restorative practices?

HEALING

I had to wrestle with the residue.

Something amazing happened as I took respite and rested. I began to think more clearly. I asked myself self-critical questions. What was my role in selecting and aligning myself in these spaces, relationships, and institutions? Why had I ignored or accepted that these places were toxic, disorienting, or distracting me from reaching purposeful alignment? What was my contribution in this situation? In my Big Mama voice, the answer came: "You picked them."

I had to come to terms with the fact that I had not done the deep healing necessary for me to purposefully align, to move into a forward stance, to find my rhythm, to focus my energy, and to have clear awareness. This time of respite and healing created an amazing opportunity to drop down into that space. I knew I couldn't take this baggage with me and move towards purposeful alignment. Like any good organizer, I started to assemble my circle of influence, my truth tellers. You know the ones who won't lie to you and won't allow you to lie to yourself. Then, I returned to my therapist, whom I had called upon several times in the previous months. I was grateful she welcomed me back with a big smile and a hug.

"Now, let's get to the hard work you were resistant to doing," she said. "If you do it, Tracey, it will open up so many amazing possibilities for you."

I also retained a chiropractor to help with the pain in my neck, shoulder, and back. I had normalized these aches from the eight years of commuting three hours, and sometimes more, each day. Funny thing is I rarely drive two hours a month now because I know that is not the normal rhythm for my body, and I embraced a better way to do the work. While I was doing the work of activating my community, nesting, organizing, and scheduling, I heard Erykah Badu singing "Bag Lady" in my head.

I had to get intimate with what it meant to let go of my baggage and make the choice to pack light going forward. This was a requirement for me to be purposefully aligned. Packing light was new to me. I had to experiment. I even changed the type of purse I carried. I traded my oversized bag, which I loved, for a simple clutch pocketbook with a long, thin strap that I could wear across my body. I could only fit the necessities in there—a few cards and dollar bills, a little change, lip gloss, and my phone—and I instantly noticed I had less clutter. Even my left shoulder, which I'd had problems with since the previous year, stopped throbbing as much. I felt lighter. Leaving the house was less of a chore. Moving from one place to the next had an ease to it.

Although I had simplified my movements, for some reason I could not calm the chatter in my head. I tried several meditation and mindfulness apps, and none of them worked. The incessant noise of constant thinking was getting in the way of my clarity. I knew the next step was to fully surrender to this journey and try something different.

As I stood in line at the UPS Store to send a package, I was struck by a laminated colorful sign hanging over the copier. It promoted a Tai Chi program. I had heard of Tai Chi, but I didn't know what it was. My only reference point was the energy therapy sessions I had taken. But this seemed different. Later, I looked up some options, and River Flow Holistic Center jumped out immediately. It was forty-five minutes away, which seemed much too far a drive for a class like that. Then, I remembered I had driven an hour and a half, daily, for eight years to carry out my life's work. I wasn't about to let a forty-five-minute drive, once or twice a week, deter my transformation process.

From the moment I walked in, I knew this was it. I committed to moving my body every day, breathing, silencing the chatter in my brain, noticing life in a new way, walking in nature, and putting another new tool and practice in a toolbox I hadn't known existed. As the days progressed, I became more familiar with the movements and the gentle instruction of my Tai Chi teacher. I constantly heard her voice in my head: "Tracey, if you do not take care of you and center yourself, you cannot help others in the world. You are being called into something bigger. You can't do it if you are not your whole, healed, and centering self."

As you lean in to transformation, give yourself permission to ask:

1. What do I need to address, interrupt, or discard to move one step closer to healing for purposeful alignment?

2. What empowering thinking do I need to embrace?

3. What empowering feelings do I need to step into?

4. What empowering actions do I need to take?

5. What new tools and community members do I need to explore at this phase of my journey?

Scan QR code above for additional questions to help embrace
respite and healing.

TRANSFORMATION PRINCIPLE 3:

CENTER YOURSELF

I had to move myself from the fringes of my life to the center in order to get proximal to transformation and move towards purposeful alignment.

My friend Robin often said, "The state of your purse and the state of your car say a lot about you." She was right. Every time I saw Robin, she was put together, polished, and humble as could be. She wasn't afraid to ask the hard questions, and she was known for saying exactly what was on her mind. About a year after I met her at the salon, she stopped me as I entered the bustling beauty shop. She stood armed with other women by her side as an intervention team.

"It's been a year now since you had that little guy," she said, referring to my son, Caleb. "It's time to get back to you. We don't want to see you come back in here wearing sweatpants ever again."

What could I do but listen? This was my circle of influence, doing a much-needed intervention. Every time I saw Robin, she would say, "Let me inspect that purse." I knew it was coming, but still, I was never prepared for it.

"Your purse is an outward expression of how you feel about yourself and your life," she'd say with a smile. "It reveals whether things are chaotic, harmonious, or downright crazy in your personal relationships, your work, or your walk." Robin told me a woman's purse reveals whether she is balanced, aligned, or just trying to make it from day to day.

The single most important relationship that needs a solid footing is that of you with yourself.

The process of centering is such a foreign concept for many people tackling complex social issues and facilitating change because we've never done it. You are making the decision to put yourself in the center of the action, your life, and your relationships. In this moment, you begin to shine a light on what you need. Centering is in direct opposition to what you have been taught or seen modeled by elders and leaders. Centering doesn't align with what you have accepted as necessary to facilitate change, what's needed to do the heavy lifting in the work of building strong communities, institutions, and relationships. However, the single most important relationship that needs a solid footing is that of you with yourself. And centering helps you to develop that relationship.

The work of impacting complex social change begins with a narrative built upon self-sacrifice, continuous giving, and putting the needs of others before your own. That behavior of constantly shrouding your needs in a narrative of humbleness, pride, and undying commitment can be tiring and self-defeating. This unfortunate yet common phenomenon often shows up as burnout, neglect of your body and family, and ultimately, illness, disease, or death. I had it bad.

The process of moving myself from the fringes of my life—where I buried myself in my work and neglected myself and my relationships—to putting me first, was difficult. On one hand, the decision to shift my focus represented an important demarcation of a set of hard nos and new yeses. I was forcing myself to set new boundaries that I wasn't quite sure about. This space offered a new type of trepidation and marked a new transition. I had decided to change how I would relate to everything and everyone around me. This extreme transition exposed a vulnerability needed to bring my best self to every relationship, interaction, and situation. At the same time, it forced a new type of grieving that allowed me to let go of what had been and embrace what was yet to come.

GET PROXIMAL

Transformation is not possible without further interrogation and examination.

This practice of centering created the necessity to get proximal to myself and to more intimately explore my dreams, my desires, and the relationships that mattered most to me. I wasn't prepared to do this type of work, but it came to me like a blazing fire. Proximity—getting situated close to the point of origin—is anchored in authenticity, allowing you to ask questions that examine what needs to be amplified and interrupted. The answers open the door to then ask what can be reimaged in support of purposeful alignment.

Proximity requires interrogation to shine a light on things not easily seen. You draw upon courage to go deeper within yourself, unleashing a significant level of discomfort, gratitude, and reflection. All of these are necessary components to surrender to the power of permission and transformation. The examination of proximity must happen at three levels: 1) exploring your authentic self, 2) dismantling the stories you tell yourself about yourself, and 3) deconstructing the stories others tell about you.

✳ ✳ ✳

"Hey, superstar, what are you doing?" Veronica asked on our phone call. She was always in tune with where I was. I definitely didn't feel like a superstar, but this was her way of making me chuckle.

"I'm trying to get my plan together to get clear," I replied. "I have to get things moving."

It had been less than sixty days since my departure from the life I had built and nearly suffocated under. But it felt like six months. Hearing myself speak those words, I realized the healing wasn't complete. I still felt as if I needed to do something more. I needed to prove to others—and to myself—my ongoing commitment to important work, that I wasn't slacking, or lazy, or uncaring. However, my rest was incomplete.

"Relax, Tracey. You're right where you're supposed to be. You're doing the work you are supposed to be doing at this moment." Her voice was soothing and her words reassuring. "We're helping you protect this space, but you have to be willing to own it, sit in it, and enjoy it."

I was reminded that centering myself and creating proximity allowed for a type of surrendering to the process, in which I understood this was sacred space. This was my space. I had to own it unapologetically. I had to choose how I was going to use it. Thankfully, this new space became my haven, where I didn't have to explain. All I needed to do was just be. Those who loved me saw me and gave me grace to take the time to embrace the moment in my own way. I had to submerge myself in a transformational process of experimentation. Testing the waters was a luxury I didn't previously have time for outside of CoThinkk and my work. Truth be told, I didn't allow myself the opportunity to even entertain certain things. Previously, I saw this as a luxury I just didn't have. But in this space, it was critical.

I confronted the following questions that you might also consider:

1. Who in my circle of influence do I need to call on to help me adjust my posture and center myself?

2. What do I like to do? What did I used to do or like that I no longer do?

3. What things or people make me smile?

4. What spaces and new activities make my body feel right?

5. When I am doing my best work, what am I doing?

Scan QR code above for additional questions to explore as you center yourself.

* * *

Ultimately, creating an interesting cocktail of exciting emotions, and at the same time, disempowering thinking, forced me to push up against the self-imposed narratives constantly forming in mind. Was it okay for me to take this time? Was I making a mistake? Headhunters reached out to me left and right with what would have once seemed like ideal opportunities. Listening to voicemail messages from search firms, pitching dream jobs, and reading job descriptions created a level of tension within my body. They all seemed to jumble together like alphabet soup. As I interrogated each opportunity, I thought, "This is too much for one person to do. This will take me away from my family. I won't have any balance. This can't be the only way to have impact."

I sat at the edge of my bed, quiet. About an hour and three Tylenol tablets later, I realized I had to give myself full permission to explore the idea that I could have just as much (or greater) impact doing my work a different way. I had worked for decades within the system and outside the system. What would it look like to work on the fringes and outside of the system without working inside? What additional tools would I need? What relationships would be required? How could I widen my vision of what this work could be? With this awareness also came fears. What if I embrace doing my work differently and I become less impactful, even invisible? Can I afford this financial risk? Is it really a risk at all, or am I projecting that? I needed a lifeline.

I called my friend, Anita, and I was so excited to hear her voice. Anita is a patient listener, constantly processing and taking in information. After the usual laugher and pleasantries of our conversation, plus a good measure of beating around the bush, I finally got to the point and asked, "Should I stay in this space or seriously explore this new opportunity to evolve who I am in my career? Do you think I'm missing out on an opportunity?"

Without skipping a beat, Anita calmly said, "This position is not your work." Her tone was as matter-of-fact as my mother's was when sharing one of her simple Southern sayings. "I see you now, Tracey, and I only see happiness. There is a calmness and a joy about you that I haven't seen in a long time." I was near tears as she continued. "I've seen you unhappy, and it broke my heart. I like this space where you are, Tracey." Her tone lifted. "You can always decide to take a job, but this moment right now is about you being true to where you are and what you desire to do as your work. Opportunities will come and go. You won't miss out on anything."

I needed to hear that. I took a deep breath, one of those that comes from the pit of your stomach. I realized then, and I'm not ashamed to say, that I needed her permission, along with that of my circle of influence, to take my next step. I needed their support, their faith in me, and their encouragement. I also needed to give myself permission to do what was right for me at that critical time.

As you lean in to transformation, give yourself permission to ask:

1. What fears to do I need to overcome to center myself and to get proximal to transformation?

2. Who in my circle of influence do I need permission, support, or affirmation from to lean solidly in to this space?

3. What disempowering thinking, feelings, and actions do I need to interrupt?

4. What empowering thinking, feelings, and actions do I need to embrace and adopt?

TRANSFORMATION PRINCIPLE 4:

RETOOL AND EXPERIMENT

SEE WITH FRESH EYES

Retooling is the process of releasing old tools or skills that no longer serve you well and adopting new ones. Retooling shows up in so many ways, from new strategies and approaches to new networks, resources, and risk-taking. Learning this concept of retooling was an opportunity for me to imagine what was possible in my work. It was like having the opportunity to see my life's work through a pair of fresh eyes. I wanted it, and I knew I needed some help to begin this critical process.

From the moment I learned about the Design Sprint workshop, I wanted in on it, and I was determined to do whatever it took to attend. The cost was out of range for me, but I managed to negotiate with the organizers to let me be a part of it at a very discounted rate. I was fascinated by the concept of speeding up the processing that could lead to big visions, solutions, and ideas. This class was exactly what I needed to dive deeper into this work. As I sat at a table with city planners and designers, figuring out how to adapt the design sprint strategy as a new tool to support the work that I hadn't yet envisioned, I pushed the presenters on their thinking regarding equity. My questions came lightning fast and probably caught them off guard. "How would you need to adjust the process to ensure decisions are made using an equity lens? What are the prompts that need to be baked into the process to ensure intentional equity choice points are considered?"

The presenters were appreciative of the questions and named it as a tension in their model that they hadn't quite resolved. During a brief break, we continued the discussion and began to name areas for consideration to raise important questions. I left the training with new connections, pondering new thoughts and experimenting with new tools and new questions.

Slowly but surely, with every experiment, either with a new tool or a new relationship, this new "whatever it was going to be" slowly revealed itself. Each addition to the whole made the process more and more like assembling a five thousand-piece puzzle. The good thing was I didn't have to control the parts. I could move them, interrogate them, or put them into play at my leisure. There was no pressure, no expectation. The only requirement was for me to lean in to this space, to notice and analyze, to accept the good, to remove the bad, and to decide what felt right for me. The process allowed me to ask critical questions without the pressure to resolve them all.

You might also be grappling with questions such as these. If so, just sit with them. The answers will come.

1. What is my role and responsibility at this moment?

2. What ongoing healing and acceptance from myself do I need in order to fully lean in to this moment?

3. What would it look like to bring all of me to the table?

I STOPPED MAKING PEOPLE BLURRY

In addition to the process of adding new resources and skill sets to your toolkit, you also have to be willing to let go of coping mechanisms, skills, and perspectives that no longer serve you on this journey. This was a critical process for me as I reexamined a special skill set, I had learned and honed over the years as one of my superpowers.

Everyone has an arsenal of superpowers. One of mine is making people blurry. Well, it used to be. Someone could be standing right in front of me, and I had the uncanny ability to make them blurry. They literally became blurry from head to toe until they eventually disappeared in front of my eyes. I used to be proud of this gift because I thought it allowed me to navigate challenging situations or helped me deal with people who were toxic, unhealthy, or threatening.

When I revealed this to Towanna, she seemed surprised. After two days of intense coaching under Towanna at the Coach Diversity Institute training, an intensive program I participated in as one way to intentionally retool and add new skill sets to support this journey, I felt I could trust her with my secret. After she recovered from the shock, she asked me some powerful questions that forced me into deep reflection. Why did I need this gift? Was it really a gift? What tools, resources, healing, and lingering narratives had I not mastered, requiring me to develop such a skill?

TAKE OFF THE RED CAPE

Not all superpowers make you stronger. Some make you weak. Sometimes, they get in the way of you being your best self. I ultimately realized making people blurry got in the way of my full transformation. Purposely blurring out the faces and bodies of people who came in opposition to me stopped me from having an expansive lens through which I could view purposeful alignment and support transformational leaders. Without the conscious shift to surrender this tool, I would not have been able to address conflict immediately. I would not have adopted an evolved solution-focused approach to conflict that resists the act of putting individuals into boxes that generate inaccurate and false narratives and cause me take things personally.

Giving up my superpower enhanced my ability to lead with compassion. This truly was a leveling-up moment. I could consistently anchor my actions by modeling a way of being that harnesses the collective power of others and builds leaderful organizations and movements. The combination of compassion and respect helps set clear expectations, tap into the strengths and passions of others, and move partners, colleagues, and allies into positions that leverage their best strengths, yielding greater impact. Had I held on to my superhuman ability to make people blurry, I would not have been prepared to level up in important moments and provide intentional support, coaching, and resources to the people who needed them most. Nor would I have been able to communicate often, consistently, and openly with the goal of moving others forward without allowing distraction or paralyzing impactful efforts.

Had I continued in my work without the benefit of retooling, I would not have known my non-negotiables, those aspects of my life that are not open for discussion, debate, or the opinions of others. Nor would I have fostered the ability to align with my personal and professional values. Without a doubt, retooling showed me I could give myself permission to stop and practice self-care, which includes permission to reset, seek respite, and reflect.

By embracing retooling as a proxy for activating transformation, I was ultimately able to interrupt the false belief that transformation is traumatic. Taking off my red superhero cape to embrace retooling and boldly reimagining what could be possible was liberating. Everything I needed to know would be revealed if I remained open to all possibilities and explored every one of them. If I said yes and stayed curious, if I continued to ready myself by strategically retooling, if I created clarity by wrapping myself in an amazing community, I couldn't fail. This intense, rapid movement towards a desired vision of purposeful alignment is cyclical, not linear. The ongoing work, therefore, is restorative and prepares you for what is next.

As you lean in to transformation, give yourself permission to ask:

1. What is my superpower?

2. What am I fighting for?

3. Is my superpower serving me well in this moment?

4. What does it look like to do this work differently? Where? With whom? How?

5. What do I need to stop, challenge, resist, or embrace in my transformational journey?

6. What new relationships, new community members, and new skills do I need?

Scan QR code above for additional questions on how to retool and experiment.

Let's dream out loud together and begin to imagine what your first yes would be as you lean in to transformation. Use the diagram below to identify your first yes. Then, imagine what you think your three nos would need to be to support your first yes.

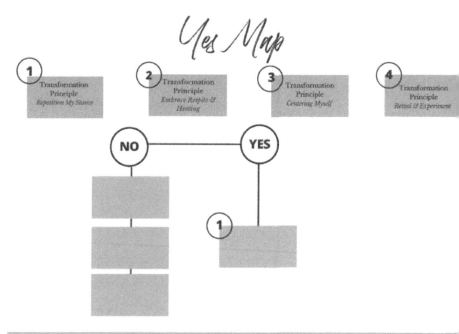

CHOICE 3:

BECOME A GAME CHANGER

This is the time to change the game, as in the lyrics of India Arie in "Just Do You."

MOVE FROM STRETCHING TO BEING A GAME CHANGER

It was time to level up and the challenge excited me.

Stretching is an intentional act to extend yourself beyond perceived limits. You choose to take a forward-facing posture to address the complexities of social change with an eye towards having greater impact. You step into being a game changer and being purposefully aligned. Then, comes an important challenge you cannot avoid—to remain balanced in your efforts, while holding just enough healthy tension against a backdrop that allows for full transformation. This type of stretching is not only a response to the actual transformation taking place, it is the required heavy lifting you must do every day to support the most critical piece of this puzzle—cultivating, building, modeling, and sustaining healthy, positive, and equitable relationships. All of this is necessary to prepare you to embrace your game-changer status.

By moving from a posture of stretching to being a game changer, you position yourself to choose a reset towards purposeful alignment. As a game changer, you are intentional in aligning your values with your actions. You solidly anchor yourself in your faith to reach your desired state. Your ultimate goal is to move from success to significance.

Being a game changer requires a commitment to self-discovery, and by continuing to grow and deepen your relationships, you create an environment for more impactful work. Embracing the posture of game changer allows you to create new models, new tools, and new processes. You enhance your ability to develop more critical initiatives, to embrace lessons learned, and to gain clarity regarding leadership. Your perspective on collaboration, non-negotiables, and various roles in leading and facilitating critical social change is thereby expanded.

Game changer status requires intentional space to engage the hard questions of alignment and impact and the juxtaposition of gifts and talents against a complex backdrop. It requires an unwavering desire to model compassionate leadership, transparency, and vulnerability. You strengthen your skills of active listening, flexibility, patience, asking powerful questions, and impact in addressing complex issues. Among these issues are equity, systems change, movement, and catalyzing ecosystems of change.

Your ultimate goal is to move from success to significance.

Game-changer status leans into hard discussions of shifting narratives, sharing power, and transforming to thrive. This transition represents a pivotal moment of significant transition where you are being presented with new opportunities that deepen your work. Then, you can embrace transformation as an ongoing process that grows stronger. As you move forward, you adopt an unwillingness to remain silent and invisible. All your actions are bold and strategically carry a level of big risk. You intentionally rest and reset when needed and return to your work laser-focused on initiatives aligned with your values. This is a necessary and bold posture you must embrace to move from successful work to significant, life-changing, legacy-building work.

As you become a game changer, give yourself permission to ask:

1. Am I ready to be a game changer?

2. What might significance look like to me? Significant to whom? Why?

3. Am I ready to move from success to significance?

4. What is holding me back?

5. Who in my circle of influence will be with me along this journey?

Scan QR code above for additional questions to explore as you become a game changer.

You are well prepared to move into Game Changer position. Here is what you can expect:

- Game-Changer Principle 1: Reset Your Narrative

- Game-Changer Principle 2: Reintroduce Yourself

- Game-Changer Principle 3: Celebrate

GAME-CHANGER PRINCIPLE 1:

RESET YOUR NARRATIVE

The old narratives no longer served me, so I had to reset and reintroduce myself.

There I was, sitting at the head of a rectangular mahogany table, talking to members of the hiring committee. I had received an email outlining a very succinct schedule with specific topics regarding the flow of the interview. As I began the interview with the six-member search committee, I immediately shifted the flow from an interview to a conversation. I acknowledged the email and respectfully declined the structure. I then presented an alternative to frame the conversation I wanted to have about what was required for me to seriously consider the opportunity. "This conversation is about whether this opportunity is a good fit for both of us," I said confidently. "For me, it is about organizational readiness for and alignment with a vision and culture that anchors deeply in my values of equity, networks, process, and collaboration." I felt more empowered with each word I spoke. "This conversation is about whether we can all have the impact we desire."

They leaned back in their chairs and conceded to the new structure, and we began a meaty discussion without any artificial filters or barriers. We moved from a very superficial conversation to a more in-depth one that acknowledged the challenge ahead and the strategies, opportunities, and blind spots. In that moment, I chose the new narrative I was going to carry into this space. I decided how I would show up, and I was explicit about the need for alignment, without hesitation or trepidation. I rejected the old story, in which I would hold back and only bring parts of myself into the process. My previous, misaligned self would have felt the need to explain the importance of CoThinkk in my life and move with caution when asking hard questions. In this significant moment, I chose to reset the narrative about how I would show up here and any future spaces in a way that supported my decision to be purposefully aligned. With that choice, I brought my full self to the table.

Awareness of your story's true narrative, along with the choice to reset it, is vital and is an integral part of your transformational process. This is critical to moving into a game-changer posture. The story and the narrative you portray to others may look different from the reality of your real narrative. Your authentic narrative is for your eyes only, at least at first. You eventually will have to choose to share it to move into purposeful alignment, but it is for you, first and foremost. Your narrative includes a series of related events and experiences—essentially, stories—that can be either true or fictitious. The true stories describe actual events you have experienced. The fictitious stories help you visualize what you want for yourself in the future. Each of your stories has five basic and equally important elements: The characters, the setting, the plot, the conflict, and the resolution.

CHARACTERS

The characters in your narrative are the individuals that the story is about, and they are easily pointed out with identifying information, detailed descriptions of physical attributes, and personality traits. In your narrative, you are the main character and are able to determine the way the plot develops, how problems are solved, and which supporting characters you will enlist to provide additional details, explanations, or actions to move the story along.

SETTING

The setting is the location of the action. It describes the environment or surroundings of your story in such detail that you can recall the scene clearly and vividly.

PLOT

The plot is the actual story around which the entire narrative is based. It has a very clear beginning, middle, and end and can be easily followed from start to finish.

CONFLICT

Every story has a conflict, which includes ways the characters attempt to resolve the problem with an exciting climax. The story's action becomes more exciting right before the resolution.

RESOLUTION

Lastly, the solution to the problem is the way the action is resolved. It ties in with the overall narrative to create an ending you want to manifest and experience. These essential elements keep the story running smoothly and allow the action to develop in a logical way.

In resetting your narrative, you acknowledge your stories do not always run smoothly and are heavily influenced by messages, triggers, real-life moments, other people, and the mental messages you send yourself. Ultimately, these messages reveal that you have the final choice. The ability to interrogate and shift each of these elements of your story is closely tied to your success. Ultimately, resetting your narrative is the first step for you to understand how to recreate your story, when and how to adjust your story, and how to arm yourself with tools for purposeful alignment.

As you reset your narrative and your life, give yourself permission to ask:

1. What makes me happy and energized about my narrative or story?

2. What narratives or stories do I need to let go of to shift towards purposeful alignment?

3. What old narratives or stories am I hanging on to that no longer serve me well and that I must discard?

4. What empowering thinking, feelings, and actions do I need to embrace in my narrative or story?

5. What disempowering thinking, feeling, and actions do I need to let go of in my story?

Scan QR code above for additional questions to help reset your narrative.

GAME-CHANGER PRINCIPLE 2:

REINTRODUCE YOURSELF

Some wanted the old version of me back, but she was no longer invited to the party. Others embraced the new me.

I heard familiar voices and conversations, one after another. They were colleagues I had known for years, my close team members, my supporters, my cheerleaders. Their conversations were casual, simple, matter of fact. The words weren't laced with judgment, only inquisitiveness and curious confusion threaded through each word spoken.

"She's just different now."

"I don't know who this Tracey is."

"The things she used to do before; she doesn't do anymore."

"She seems different. It's hard to describe, but I like it."

I could only grin from ear to ear as I heard their words. I heard these statements in different settings, from different voices, with different inflection points. Each time I reflected on them, I remained at peace and affirmed I was right where I was supposed to be.

An interesting thing happens when you are in this transformational process. For some people, who have not been witness to your transformation, the process seems to appear right out of thin air, like magic. For others, who have been on the journey with you, it is as if you are a butterfly emerging from a cocoon. They have patiently watched the process, celebrated every moment of the journey, offered cover to you in your most vulnerable state, and eagerly awaited the big reveal.

The reintroduction process is one of the most exciting and one of the scariest moments of your purposeful alignment journey. It is the moment when you choose to unapologetically share all of who you are with the world. It is the moment when you are either celebrated, criticized, or simply viewed as different. In this moment of reintroduction, several things quickly reveal themselves.

YOUR LEVEL OF CLARITY

I knew exactly who I was and where I wanted to go.

Your level of clarity has peaked and is clear to everyone around you. Clarity is such an amazing gift because when you are clear, you are able to make concise decisions without the need to apologize or qualify each statement. The need for approval you once had shifts to seeking counsel from your most trusted truth-tellers, those leading change most aligned with your values. In this space of clarity, you quickly drown out the voices and fear-filled opinions of others in exchange for wisdom and excitement about the future. You are drawn by a need to push beyond the boundaries, to reimagine something that has yet to be envisioned or created. The voices of those who just don't get you anymore are quickly drowned out. With ease and grace, you push them to the fringes, all the while thanking and cheering the community standing next to you, nudging you forward with love and a deep belief in who you are and what you are called do.

HEALTHY, POSITIVE, AND EQUITABLE RELATIONSHIPS

The difference between what was healthy and what was toxic became clear.

My ability to recognize, fairly quickly, the difference between toxic relationships and healthy, positive, and equitable relationships became sharper and quicker. It had been months since I began doing this work of retooling to become a game changer. In this time, I purposely created space between myself and certain people, places, and situations. I made no announcement, offered no apology, and gave no explanation. So it was no surprise to me when I received a text message from a colleague. Our last correspondence had been nearly four months prior. Her text read: "I've definitely been thinking about you and missing you, especially your attempts to contact me. I'm not sure why we haven't been able to connect."

I'm a processor, so in the past, a text like this would have made me toss and turn. I would have unpacked it a hundred times over before responding. But this time, I didn't. I responded to the text by acknowledging it and indicating I had created some healthy boundaries. The ease and truth with which I replied was confirmation that the boundary I had set was aligned with where I was. By creating this boundary, I freed space for new opportunities, new relationships, and new spaces. I knew with certainty that the healthy, positive, and equitable relationships I had decided to allow in my life had to be reciprocal. These kinds of relationships allow the space for hard conversations about difficult issues.

Healthy relationships foster the creation of intentional space and the interruption of false narratives. Positive relationships are grounded in truth. Equitable relationships resist complicity in supporting issues or practices that perpetuate inequities. These holistic relationships operate from a place of good intention and honesty without a hidden agenda. They create safe spaces that resist vilifying or rendering individuals invisible when issues get uncomfortable and hard, all while extending grace and support to face the intense change necessary to amplify collective efforts. These relationships form a rich tapestry of alliances, collaborations, and networks. When unifying relationships are formed, aligned, effective, and sustainable change is possible. Consequently, the effort to maintain the integrity of such relationships is constant and necessitates individual self-reflection, learning, and ongoing growth. Everyone involved must go deeper into self to become conscious of their own triggers, which can show up unconsciously in engagements with new individuals.

The process of becoming a game changer is not a simple one. It takes a willingness and a commitment to see change for yourself and for the whole. Retreat when needed and embrace the vulnerability that enables you to say, "I don't know. Can you be a thought partner with me?" Regroup when you feel paralyzed. Integrate lessons learned as you seek a different result or an alternative path forward. Have the courage to stand alone and model a way of being that creates a bigger table for unpopular voices allowing for more grounded, innovative, and successful strategies. Be present, be silent, and listen to and with others to see past their struggle. Acknowledge the things they have done well and challenge them to let go of what has been to dream of what could be. Know when to stop pushing. Learn to pause, encourage respite, celebrate, break bread together, and get to know each other on a deeper level beyond the present work, without trepidation or fear. Sit in the reality of the moment while balancing the vision of what it can become. Deal with the fear of being rendered invisible, discarded, and unappreciated as you tackle the hard work.

Equitable relationships resist complicity in supporting issues or practices that perpetuate inequities.

The cultivating, building, modeling, and sustaining of healthy, positive, equitable relationships must be a constant thread in your work every day. It will steady you in your most challenging moments and provide collective strength as you embrace a game changer and futurist posture that enables a sharp pivot towards greater impact. Only in this posture can you anticipate and acknowledge shifting trends and galvanize the collective towards a shared future shaped by diverse voices, new narratives, innovation, and aligned collaborations. In this way, you disrupt policies and practices that perpetuate barriers and inequities.

As you grow into this game-changing posture, grapple with these critical questions:

1. What is my struggle to nurture healthy, positive, and equitable relationships?

2. What do I need to heal to have the courage to lean in to this work?

3. What trauma do I need to face that stops me from embracing this work?

4. How will I choose to resist practices, behaviors, and strategies that hinder the impact of the stretch, even when I feel hurt, discounted, or uncertain about change?

5. What three things am I prepared to let go of this year?

6. What three things will I interrupt, innovate, and amplify today?

Your ability to have ongoing discourse about this important issue will help drive you towards the best solutions, which are necessary to create a better tomorrow for future generations.

BOUNDARIES

Like attracts like.

I had seen her in many meetings. I loved her perspective, her passion, and the way she was with people. When I talked to her, I knew she was taking it all in. I loved that she called me on the phone early in the mornings. I couldn't believe she remembered I was an early bird. I loved when we had lunch together and we talked on and on and on. She had a way about her, and I just got her. Unfortunately, my schedule was too tight to squeeze in one of our lunchtime chats. What would I need to change to make space for this new beautiful friendship?

Having clarity and becoming conscious of the types of relationships that occupy your space allows you to exercise choice. With that, you can set healthy boundaries. Mind you, boundaries are not necessarily focused on keeping people out. Boundaries help to right-size relationships in your life. Right-sizing means putting things in appropriate perspective in relationship to your entire life. It is the process of assessing investment in a specific area to ensure it is aligned with the time, gifts, energy, and commitments of other or similar investments in your life.

In order to be a game changer, you have to be willing to right-size your investments across all aspects of your life. This is how you determine what is most aligned. This is how you get clear on which items are a good fit for the new version of who you are and what no longer has a place in this new space you have created. This can be scary and also sad at times. But you must see boundaries as helpful. They allow you to renegotiate your relationships with people. They allow you to be clear about what you need. They allow you to be clear about what is required of you. They require you to accept when circumstances are out of place.

Boundaries allow you to view yourself, the world, and others in a way that enables you to make clear and strategic decisions regarding how to move forward. They allow you to attract energy, ideas, people, relationships, and new opportunities in service to purposeful alignment. Like will attract like.

As you grow into this game-changing posture, grapple with these critical questions:

1. What new boundaries do I need to put in place?

2. What right-sizing in relationships, spaces, and my career do I need to implement?

3. What disempowering thoughts, feelings, and actions do I need to interrupt regarding boundaries?

4. What empowering thoughts, feelings, and actions do I need to embrace regarding boundaries?

5. Who within your circle of influence will you have to let you go?

6. Who will move forward with you?

COMMITMENTS

I was unwilling to move the line I had drawn in the sand.

Your commitments change in this new posture. You view your commitment to embrace curiosity differently. This, in turn, enables openness, new awareness, and a sharpened ability to ask critical questions without judgment or opinion. You begin to think bigger about what is possible and ask questions that influence the thinking of others in your community. You hear in a way you have never heard before. Your attention is clear now, and you have silenced the chatter. This allows the tuning in of unrelenting truth, honesty, and authenticity.

At every step along my coaching training journey, the instructors at Coach Diversity Institute cautioned me that, in order to be a coach, I had to be coachable. Part of being coachable is hearing in a different way, listening in a different way, and being present in a different way. This new way of being affirmed me in my new role. I had clarity that my work would sit at the intersection of community economic development, health and wellbeing, leadership development, and education.

However, I did not know that, in those spaces, I would commit to toggling between three spheres of influence: 1) supporting those working directly in the system to be bolder, take risks, and push the boundaries; 2) working on the fringes of the system to push it in new ways by asking powerful questions, coaching, and serving as a strategic thought partner; and 3) working outside of the system to push new ideas, models, strategies, and approaches as a proposition to the world about how to interrupt and replace outdated practices, thinking, and structural change.

This fresh insight also encouraged me to begin intentionally caring for myself. I made the commitment to walk every day, to meditate, to do my Tai Chi practices, and to set boundaries around my time. I needed these regular practices to support the essential next step for me.

It was the beginning of November when I began to have conversations with new and existing clients about a shift in my schedule. "I'm so excited about working with each of you to advance our collective work. That said, my last day in the office will be December 15th, and I will return the second week in January."

I wanted to explain more about why I was taking the extended time off. I wanted them to understand this wasn't a self-indulgent vacation, but an unwavering commitment to self-care, balance, and purposeful alignment. But my new self wouldn't allow it. I heard my own internal voice say, "You don't have to explain, Tracey." So I held my breath and resisted the posture of self-defense as I waited for raised concern or nervousness. They never came. Finally, I exhaled. And a strange and beautiful thing happened. My clients voiced their support.

"I appreciate you setting those boundaries and creating clarity."

"We will get everything done before the second week in December."

"I'm happy to schedule time with you upon your return."

"I appreciate you being clear about your commitment to be present with your family and keeping that hard line. Thank you for allowing me to have just thirty minutes of your time. I assure you I will honor your boundaries,"

"Thank you for modeling this. I wish I would have set a boundary like this. I will model your lead and do better. I am sure my loved ones and I will appreciate it."

"I completely understand. We will wait to solidify everything the second week in January."

I had tested the space, and it revealed that this commitment was modeling something for others. I was demonstrating how to protect sacred space. Despite my concern that others would view my actions as a lack of commitment to their work, it actually made them want to work with me more. In fact, they appreciated my clarity and my unwillingness to waver in a moment when it was easy to make concessions. I felt deep gratitude for the partners, organizations, and leaders I was working with on this leg of the journey.

EXPECTANCY

Whatever you choose to do, you will be great at it.

Expectancy is the state of thinking or hoping something, especially something pleasant, will happen. In a game-changer posture, not only is your expectation level amplified, it is magnified, and becomes contagious. It compels you to move past resiliency and focus on thriving at every turn of your journey. In addition, you compel others to thrive. As you level up, you desire and intentionally act to bring everyone with you. At this point, the entire movement becomes about the collective. The expectation that everyone will thrive becomes the norm and is a non-negotiable that creates an enormous ripple, which multiplies over and over in the form of new resources, relationships, networks, and partners.

When you are in service to living a fulfilled life and to standing in your unique power, you authentically facilitate amazing change as you walk in purposeful alignment. Expectancy, then, is normalized in such a deep and tremendous way that it becomes a part of your walk, your talk, your DNA. It is manifested as a glow that is magnified in every space you enter. Many will name it, but few can articulate it. It just is.

As you grow into this game-changing posture, grapple with these critical questions:

1. What new expectations do I need to put in place for myself and for others?

2. What empowering thoughts, feelings, and actions do I need to embrace regarding expectations?

3. What disempowering thoughts, feelings, and actions do I need to interrupt regarding expectations?

4. What support and encouragement do I need from my circle of influence?

GAME-CHANGER PRINCIPLE 3:

CELEBRATE

She said I was broken open, but not broken.

When Gayle slipped away to the kitchen to prepare our tea, I snuggled into her cozy couch like an infant tucked in a mother's arms. That couch seemed to wrap itself around me in an intimate embrace. "I could sit here forever," I thought, glancing out the window at the wooded landscape that surrounded her home.

With two cups of steaming herbal tea, Gayle rejoined me on the couch, and I picked up where I had left off. I rambled on and on while Gayle sat there, sipping and smiling. She listened intently, posing a curious question here and there. Then, she lifted her face from her warm cup and said, "You were broken open, but not broken."

Although I acknowledged her observations, I did not truly understand what Gayle meant until eleven months later. As I reflected on her statement, the image of an egg balanced between two fingers instantly came to mind. When an egg is broken, the shell fractures into multiple pieces. It could break evenly into two halves or many tiny parts. But no matter how it is cracked, only the shell—the outer layer—is broken. When the shell is removed, the beautiful yellow yolk is revealed.

Months later, I realized her statement was not about being broken. It was an acknowledgement of my courage and strength. It was an awareness of my decision to level up, to evolve. It was an invitation to celebrate every lesson and experience that led me to that day. It was also a celebration of what was to come. My being broken open, but not broken, described a new level of self-awareness, a deeper place of understanding, and a clarity necessary to move me through a transformational process. And to my surprise, it was not only an internal movement, but it was apparent to those who had been watching me. That felt good.

My journey into purposeful alignment for transformational leadership required a new stance rooted in an unapologetic boldness to take risks to address complex change. It was about having a deeper awareness of self. Despite my trepidations, this journey had broken me open; it had caused an evolution in my thinking. It made me confront disempowering thoughts, feelings, and actions. It allowed me to lean in to my power and anchor in healing, the collective, collaboration, love, family, and partnerships.

SELF-CARE REDEFINED

Self-care was no longer just a practice of activities. I finally understood self-care was the act of being purposefully aligned.

I was on a Zoom call with a panel of women, all change agents, to discuss self-care for women of color. The organizer had sent us four questions to speak to as a part of the conversation. From the very first question it was clear my recent evolution had changed my perspective and voice on this issue. As I prepared for the conversation, a level of awareness washed over me, and I understood that, prior to embarking upon my journey of purposeful alignment, my answers and my contributions to this discussion would have been completely different.

Self-care is a necessity for any leader willing to endure the messy middle of transformation to emerge whole and liberated.

The question posed was, "How do you define self-care?" As I readied myself to speak, I was clear that self-care begins with embracing the power of permission. It is the understanding that you have to lean in to transformation and not run from it. Self-care encompasses the commitment to adjust your stance to become a game changer. It is at the core of the decision to create a new narrative that includes purposeful alignment as a non-negotiable. Self-care is a necessity for any leader willing to endure the messy middle of transformation to emerge whole and liberated.

By resisting and denying purposeful alignment in my own life, I had inadvertently been unkind to myself and modeled that behavior for others around me. I was complicit in my ongoing trauma. I was harming myself. I was perpetuating practices, behaviors, and relationships that suggested a level of normalcy, but were, in fact, abnormal. I was creating a space where bringing all of me was not the norm. By redefining self-care as purposeful alignment, I put in place important choice points that defined my new normal.

AMPLIFY CHOICE POINTS

In my work, I constantly challenge individuals, leaders, institutions, and communities to get clear about their choice points. Complex change work requires intentional conversations about the power of choice points in every aspect of our efforts. Amplifying your choice points is an important part of critical decisions that influence outcomes and create a clear line of sight for your why. According to Race Forward, a national movement for racial justice and part of the Center for Social Inclusion, choice points are even more powerful when coupled with prompts, reminders you intentionally put in place to keep your line of sight clear. Prompts are clear, concrete, and poignant nudges you put in place to reconnect to power, continue to do your work, and reflect to keep your why front and center.

These prompts serve as crucial levers that force you to continue to plant important seeds in three critical areas: 1) your mental models, assumptions, beliefs, and biases; 2) your physical state of health; and 3) your spiritual connection or flow. All three work in tandem in service to raising your vibrations—the energy and momentum unique to your vision and calling—and allowing you to align, reset, and lean in to your natural flow.

Being intentional about the choices you make in resetting your story to usher in the new helps you avoid traveling the same path you have traveled before. If you do find yourself on a previous path, your awareness is heightened, and you are better able to quickly course correct. Consequently, you get to envision a new path by making strategic and powerful choices that feel natural for you. Embracing this level of mindfulness allows you to lean in to your game-changer posture. You develop and embrace emergent practices and iterative processes to embrace your new story and ushering in the new.

As you grow into this game-changing posture, grapple with these critical questions:

1. What choice points do I need to amplify?

2. Which options generate the most leverage, intent, and momentum towards purposeful alignment?

3. Is there an experience in my narrative that may be unintentionally reinforcing an old story that has been holding me back?

4. What are the impacts of current decisions and actions that may be unintentionally reinforcing biases and barriers from old narratives that no longer serve me?

5. Who in my circle of influence will be my accountability partner as I practice these new choices and prompts?

Scan QR code above for additional questions as you let go of the old and usher in the new.

THE COMING-OUT PARTY

The moment had arrived.

For weeks, I practiced, day in and day out. Each morning I found myself practicing my talk, over and over, to the rhythm of my feet walking the winding sidewalks of our neighborhood. I practiced my breathing and voice inflections while driving from one appointment to another. Even with all of that, I didn't feel prepared for the level of intensity required to stand on that infamous red dot to deliver a TEDx talk.

I had gone through at least seventeen versions of my talk, wordsmithing, editing, accepting collective feedback from my colleagues in the lineup. I thought about it every waking hour and minute of every day. On my morning walks, I mulled it over in my head. *Is that the way I want to say it?* I had to make sure I told the story accurately to honor everyone. I had no time to be bashful or to second guess myself. I had to be bold and say everything I wanted to say. I refused to have any regrets. This moment was being gifted to me to challenge others to push their thinking, to serve as a provocateur, to ask the "what if" questions. I wanted everyone to hold the possibility of what could be different in our collective thinking, feelings, and actions. It was my coming-out party, and I was ready when the light shone brightly on me.

Thankfully, I was not standing there by myself. To the right was my circle of influence. To the left were my friends, colleagues, and family. At center was my CoThinkk family. Underneath my feet was the possibility of that famous red dot which represented all the ancestors standing with me; their energy, their voices, their love, and their vibrations created tingling sensations beneath my feet as I delivered my speech. To my sheer pleasure, my talk, "Addressing Complex Social Change . . . What If?" was warmly received. As I stepped off the stage, I was hopeful that it would spark an important conversation about transforming philanthropy and reimagining what could be possible for communities through our collective work.

My coming-out party was all about embracing visibility, but not from an arrogant or normative place. This wasn't about me. It was about raising the visibility of everyone, every desire, every dream, every wish. It was about setting the stage for what was to come and planting powerful seeds about what would be, moving forward. It was about letting go of the old and embracing the new.

As you grow into this game-changing posture, grapple with these critical questions:

1. What does coming out look like for me?

2. Who in my circle of influence will be standing with me?

3. What shadows or filters do I still have to overcome to surrender to purposeful alignment?

4. What disempowering thoughts, feelings, and actions do I need to interrupt to raise my vibrations towards purposeful alignment?

5. What empowering thoughts, feelings, and actions do I need to embrace my coming-out party and maintain my forward stance?

THE YES MAP

Let's dream out loud together and begin to imagine what your first yes would be as you lean in to your game-changer posture. Use the diagram below to identify your first yes. Then, imagine what you think your three nos would need to be support your first yes.

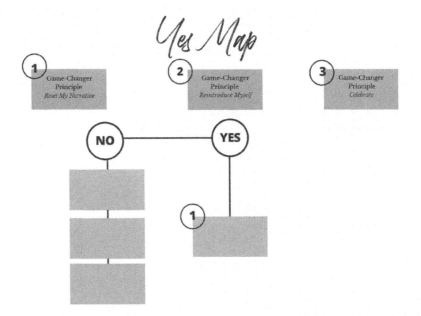

THE INVITATION

Image courtesy of Non Profit Changemakers, TopNonProfits, Graphic recording by Minds Eye Creative.

Accept the invitation to something that has yet to reveal itself, as in the lyrics from "Golden" by Jill Scott.

THEY SAID I WAS COURAGEOUS

The final tweaks to the press release were complete. It was the conclusion of the very intimate dance of my leaving an organization, where I had been a key player for close to two years, and moving into something new, something unknown. I documented on paper the key wins and impacts I had accumulated during my tenure there. At the same time, I weighed the impact of the public message explaining my transition. Thankfully, the process was polite. It had an ease to it. It felt right.

Over the months I had considered making this move, it became very clear to me that I was doing the right work in the wrong place. The culture and approach to change were not well aligned with the internal compass that had developed and matured within me over the course of my career; therefore, I had to interrupt this path. This internal compass was informed by the voices of community leaders, mentors, family, peers, and influential leaders. These were the influencers who shaped my path and continued the work to innovate and evolve ways to address complex social change.

You are positioned in these spaces to move this work forward not to take up space.

I could hear Elder Johnnie Hayes saying, "If you don't know where you are from, how do you know where you are going?"

I could hear my mother saying, "Speak up if you have something to say. If not, don't get angry if nothing is done about it."

I could hear Bernie Mazyck, Liz Santagati, Pearlie McCoy, and the King sisters from South Carolina saying, "You have to center grassroots voices. You have to make intentional space and room. It is a privilege to be invited into this work. Honor that."

I could hear Jennifer Henderson, Irvin Henderson, and Ajulo Othow saying, "It's not about you. This is one of the biggest and most important lessons you will get in this work. And we need you to get it."

I could hear Laddie Howard saying, "If you don't understand the politics, the dance, the undercurrents of this work, you will get lost and the community will lose."

I could hear Sue Berkowitz saying, "It does not matter what your intentions are. If you don't produce, it won't matter. It will be all talk."

I could hear Karl Stauber saying, "What is the impact you desire to drive and make? What are you prepared to do and called to do?"

I could hear Jim Richardson, Mario Gutierrez, Rodney Fernandez, and Gayle Williams saying, "This is not a time to be a reluctant leader. It's time to move up. This is your moment."

I could hear Bettie Hodges, Resea Willis, and Charles Stewart saying, "We cannot fail. Failure is not an option."

I could hear Gladys Washington, Linetta Gilbert, Susan Batten, and Marcus Walton saying, "The time is now. Either you move or move out of the way. Courageous leadership is needed, and we have to stand in the gap, shine light on these invisible spaces, and move this work from out of the shadows."

I could hear Leslie Winner saying, "I push you because I believe in you and I see what you don't yet see. You have the power to change it."

I could hear Anita Brown-Graham saying, "Who are you? It is time to stop hiding and dimming your light. We are ready for you, and this is your work to do."

I could hear Virgil Smith asking, "What is holding you back?"

I could hear Abdul Rasheed, Andrea Harris, and Sue Perry Cole saying, "Your job is to do no harm. You are positioned in these spaces to move this work forward, not to take up space."

I could hear Aundra Wallace, Shirley Lewis, and Robert Cooks saying, "Being strategic is not bad. Don't let it paralyze you. Allow it to

CHOOSING PURPOSEFUL ALIGNMENT

create greater impact and influence at a higher level. Be unapologetic in your efforts."

I could hear Erin Byrd asking, "What posture are you choosing, and where are you choosing to use your energy? You have a choice."

I could hear William Buster, Lavastian Glenn, Tara Kenchen, Donna-Marie Winn, Savi Horne, Mikki Sager, Bill Bynum, and Ivye Allen saying, "We are the ones standing in this moment. What are we prepared to do?"

I could hear Anton Gunn saying, "You can't wait for permission. You have to make your approach to change the norm."

I could hear Katrina Hutchins saying, "The moment is here, and you cannot be disobedient to the walk in front of you."

I could hear Veronica Hemmingway saying, "When you stop denying what's in front of you, what seeds you have planted, you will move."

I could hear Mebane Rash saying, "You don't have to kill yourself in the midst of doing this work. We need you to continue to be in this space. It can be amazing and not damaging. Life is way too short."

I could hear Tasha Ganthier saying, "Just wait for it. All will be revealed."

I could hear Stephanie Swepson Twitty, Darcel Eddins, and Desiree Adaway saying, "You don't have to surrender your power, your voice, and what you know to be true to do this work in a powerful and relentless way. The Universe will shift, and we are all here to support you."

I could hear my CoThinkk family saying, "Let's continue to be bold. Let's innovate. Let's be relentless. Our communities are counting on us to hold this space."

I could hear Cynthia Brown's voice: "I'm counting on all of you to show up. This is an important moment in time. We can't get this wrong, and we can't be disoriented and distracted. You have been positioned for this important moment today, right now, in this second."

I could hear my husband, Edmund Washington, asking, "Who are you being called to be in this moment, Tracey? You have been preparing for this moment. The choice is yours."

The culmination of these voices reverberated in my ears and ushered me forward. With every stroke of the keyboard, as I typed my final farewells, my breath slowed, my heart calmed, and my spirit settled as I leaned in to this important decision. Their voices had echoed in my ears at every moment of doing the complex and heavy work I had adopted as my life's purpose and calling, the work of influencing and driving change, justice, movement building, and equity. This moment was no exception. These voices were my constant anchor that I toggled back to as I provided my final edits to the press release. They strengthened me as I resisted the urge to say exactly what I would be doing and where I would be going.

I surrendered to what I thought, at the moment, was discomfort in not naming my plan. I now know that was the liberation of starting a powerful faith walk that would not be influenced by succinct, politically correct statements meant to create comfort for those I was leaving behind. What I knew was words matter. The power of spoken and written words could alter, reframe, and shift what was in store for me on this journey. I was unwilling to take this risk as I moved forward. And so, the press release read: "I'm reaching out today with bittersweet news. Tracey Greene-Washington announced she will be leaving for a new adventure."

THE MOMENT

The press release was posted. I'd sent a more intimate note to close friends and colleagues, but the big announcement was sent out to everyone. I resisted the urge to check my email. Instead, I settled into the calm of the moment and posted my announcement on social media. I held my breath. And then came the influx of emails, instant messages, and phone calls from friends and colleagues. Some I had deep connections with, others I had only met briefly.

Three themes emerged from the correspondences:

1) Thank you for your work, impact, and support;

2) Thank you for modeling and being a leader in this space with us and inviting us to be bold and innovative in this work; and

3) Thank you for your courage and bravery to step into a new adventure, a new space, and a new way of doing this work. We can't wait to watch the journey and see where you land. We know it will be wonderful.

I was overwhelmed with emotion and appreciative of the support. I didn't know I had so many allies cheering me on, so many people in solidarity with me, watching me, trusting me with the work. I'd had my head down for so long, just doing the daily grind of the work, that I hadn't looked up much to notice who had been watching me. My eyes welled with appreciation for being present in that moment, to let it wash over me, and to use it as a cue to just be. At the same time, immense chatter emerged in my head as I held a full-blown discussion with me, myself, and I about the reality that I didn't feel courageous at all.

My mind told me this was a new space for me. I felt unbalanced with limited clarity regarding what the exact blueprint would look like as I moved forward. I realized I was at the beginning of my process and had not created the intentional space to be still, to be vulnerable, to contemplate, to center myself. In the past, I had not valued the creation and the mining of that sacred space. This realization was the activation of my journey to ensure purposeful alignment. The journey would force me to navigate a messy and muddy pathway that moved me from Permission to Transformation, from Transformation to Game Changer, and from Game Changer to Purposeful Alignment.

CREATE A CLEAR LINE OF SIGHT TO PURPOSE

As I reflect on this journey, several lessons have been revealed in such a clear way as critical components of accepting such an important invitation. As I navigated from that moment to the ongoing journey to maintain this walk, the following lessons emerged as a means to create a focused and clear line of sight to purpose.

LESSON 1: SET INTENTION

"I have had to learn that my voice has value. And if I don't use it, what's the point of being in the room?" ~Michelle Obama

Setting intention is the foundational component of the purposeful alignment invitation. Your intentions should include creating a practice of being present, unlearning and relearning, and course correcting as needed. It should include a list of all your promises to yourself and to others in this process, your desires, and your wishes as it pertains to the outcomes, and most importantly, an investment in the intentional work of purposeful alignment.

Arguably, setting intentions, creating intentional space for courageous conversations, raising your vibrations, and leaning in to your flow go hand in hand. These are the final four key elements necessary to accept the invitation to center purposeful alignment in your life and work. One without the others does not allow for the heavy lift necessary to build intentional practices on a transformational journey that is sustainable and impactful. Creating intentional space along your journey allows for the shifting of thinking and daily schedules to create seamless practice and multiple entry points for support, structure, and clear communication that extend beyond current relationships, situations, and boundaries.

LESSON 2: CENTER COURAGEOUS CONVERSATIONS

"I am deliberate and afraid of nothing." ~Audre Lorde

There I was, in conversation after conversation with individuals, change agents, leaders, and neighbors as they examined their role, purpose, and place, and the impact they desired to leave behind over the course of their lives and careers. In each conversation, I stepped back, reflected, and processed. As my colleague Gary Hubbell would say, "I gave it time to breathe." I couldn't help but finish the ends of their sentences as they paused to ponder multiple thoughts.

"It sounds like you are seeking purposeful alignment." Without hesitation or trepidation, in every conversation, their response was a clear yes. Moment after moment, I witnessed a series of countless courageous conversations about purposeful alignment as we dropped down into intimate and colorful dialogue prompted by a set of curious "what if" questions in response to the awareness of what was being revealed. It was powerful to witness what was possible when, in every interaction, we chose to shift courageous conversations about purposeful alignment from the fringes of our interactions to the center.

What if we view these conversations as non-negotiable in our lives and work to facilitate self-care and foundational change processes that allow for innovation, greater impact, centering of people and communities, and sharing and building of power?

What if these conversations provide permission to pause and think deeply about the puzzle pieces necessary to inform choice, cultivate thought leaders as futurists, and create leaderful organizations and movements?

What if these conversations support vertical, horizontal, and foundational impact in institutions and communities?

What if we share the belief that purposeful alignment is required for individuals, communities, and institutions to be truly successful and transformational?

Courageous conversations are a critical component of the messy middle of this collective work. They make visible the invisible spots while challenging all involved to resist complicity, embrace discomfort, and address harm and trauma. They help create a clear line of sight that must be filled with carefully crafted dialogue that serves as an important primer for change at all levels of our lives. These courageous conversations shift the mental models of deeply held beliefs, resistant biases, and shared thinking to create leaderful movements for change.

Courageous conversations are grounded in the fundamentals of beginning where people and institutions are, expecting them to move, and supporting them through the journey. This expectation creates a clear line of sight for shared understanding and consensus. It creates an acceptance that this transformational process will naturally move along two parallel tracks where this work is both an explicit outcome and an incremental process. By embracing this intentional approach, the continuum of innovation, systemic change, and design thinking creates a new vision for tomorrow. This tomorrow is grounded in the explicit values of centering self, equity, and collective solutions, and centering of people and community. This leads to sharing power to address complex social issues, building the capacity of leaders across social change movements, and unleashing our collective impact.

LESSON 3: RAISE VIBRATIONS AND TRUST YOUR FLOW

"Courage is not the absence of fear—it's inspiring others to move beyond it." ~ Nelson Mandela

I sat in the closet, on a shoe trunk I'd had since graduate school, surrounded by racks of disorderly clothes that needed to be reorganized. This was the only private space I could find in the house to talk to an important member of my circle of influence, who challenged me on our call.

"Your biggest challenge at this moment is to continue to sustain the vibrations—that electric and contagious force that you have been exuding—and to move into the place of I am," she said. "You are not *leaning* in to a game-changer posture. You *have moved* into this new space

121

and posture." I sat in silence to ponder what she was saying. "This is the last leg of your journey," she continued. "It's part of your spiritual walk."

The same is true for you. This journey to purposeful alignment is your medicine, the place where you are complete. It is the space where you are truly channeling your energy and momentum in their highest forms to achieve purposeful alignment. You are maintaining a flow—the constant of energy and balance necessary to create stability and sustainability—through the constant mining, protecting, and examination of a transformational process

This process is a part of:

- the I, your intrapersonal work;

- the We, your interpersonal work;

- the Work, your role in moving complex social change and structural change; and

- the Walk, your why, your faith walk, your partnership with community, and how you choose to model and show up.

LESSON 4: FLOW

Flow is a state in which you are aligned in a seamless way—mentally, physically, and spiritually. Flow is a sign of your renewal and ongoing commitment to honor the lessons learned and the transformational process. Here, you have to mine the good stuff on an ongoing basis. Flow requires balance, stance, and the energy to sustain them. Otherwise, you cannot raise your vibrations over and over in the face of conflict, challenge, celebrations, and obstacles presented by inside and outside forces. Flow is necessary as you get proximal to people and invite them to go even deeper within the work and with those who are most impacted by it. Flow is necessary when pushing others to embrace discomfort and do the necessary work to engage in reflective processes that support hard conversations.

Flow is necessary to hold the understanding that sustained change in communities is predicated upon individuals embracing equity, cross-sector collaboration, healthy relationship building, diverse voices, shared power, and systems change. The more aligned, equitable, and transparent these interactions are, the better and more significant the impact will be. The people are the weavers who knit these efforts together and sustain them long term. Flow is necessary to work across relationships, communities, sectors, and systems. Flow is necessary to do the heavy lifting required for a clear, deep analysis. Flow is critical to being strategic and shifting important mental models.

* * *

BEGIN YOUR JOURNEY NOW

The journey towards purposeful alignment is not for the weary, but it can be a path to renewal and impact. It takes the courage to give yourself permission to align. It takes an ongoing commitment to transformation. It takes a game-changing posture grounded in a faith walk, continued examination of your narrative and story, and sustaining your flow. It is a walk filled with many twists and turns and met with ongoing effort to do your work within three critical areas—mental, physical, and spiritual.

The purposeful alignment walk constantly challenges you to raise your vibrations—in every setting, with every person, and in every space—with the clear understanding that you occupy that unique space in that moment not by chance. Your presence in that moment is a reality which was already ordered. You must be obedient to what the moment is calling you to do.

The type of will needed to sustain you in this space requires three important elements:

1. Commit to being purposefully aligned.
2. Commit to reset where necessary.
3. Commit to your flow.

Only in this sacred space of purposeful alignment was I able to see clearly and navigate uncharted waters through an unwavering faith walk. At times, it was scary and frustrating. At other times, it offered a new level of freedom hard to put into eloquent words. I am grateful to have gained an understanding of the importance of community and being present with family and friends who have had an unwavering love and commitment. I honor those who have served as an unapologetic force in ensuring I was whole, healed, and positioned right where I needed to be in each moment along the journey. I appreciate those who created and protected space that enabled me to mind those tender spots so I could show up as my best self, think bolder, and dream bigger about what is possible. I don't have enough fingers to count the number of people who showed up for me, covered me, created space in new places for me, and vouched for me while protecting my reputational capital as I moved along this journey.

As I reflect on the power and the unrelenting force of my circle of influence, I humbly thank them and scream from the mountaintops how sacred, appreciated, and valued they are for allowing me to explore the question "What if?"

In this space of asking that critical question, I adopted new practices of intentional self-care, which included dropping down into rest and respite without apology. I learned to honor new routines that value slowing down and centering self and health to have greater impact and clarity. I am forever grateful for everyone's grace, patience, tough love, and holding space for me as I clumsily tested, and leaned in to this work.

Finally, I accepted the intentional process to interrupt old stories and narratives—you know those conversations in your head that often instill fear, paralyze you, and keep you from being bolder and fully stepping into your leadership. It's so interesting how words and fleeting thoughts can have such power over you and dictate your actions and vision for the future. Taking control over my narrative and shifting my own mental models created a strong foundation for what's to come.

In the midst of this epiphany, I learned three important lessons:

1. You are constantly resetting. The narratives that worked for you last year may not work today to align purpose.

2. Every life change requires a reset in your story to interrupt disempowering thinking, feelings, and actions, and to drop down into empowering thinking, feelings, and actions.

3. You can change your life in a way that is congruent with your new vision for the future. Intentionally becoming a game changer frees you to create a new narrative towards purposeful alignment.

YOUR FIRST YES

I extend to you a humble invitation for deeper engagement and work. It is an invitation that will challenge you to plant seeds, raise your vibrations, and embrace the new through the ongoing work to assess alignment, to reset as necessary, and to trust your flow. Be brave enough to start a conversation about purposeful alignment. Accept the invitation, and join me in this work by taking the following actions to fulfill your first three yeses.

YES 1: RESPOND TO THE FOLLOWING TWO QUESTIONS:

1. To what opportunity can you say yes in this moment?

2. What do you need to say no to?

Yes 2: Complete the Purposeful Alignment survey. This tool will allow you to see where you are in your purposeful alignment journey. We will also provide recommendations to support your efforts and support new awareness moving forward.

Your First Yes....

A valuable resource to help you discover where you are on your journey towards purposeful alignment.

https://www.indigoinnovationgroup.com/purposeful-alignment-quiz

Tracey Greene-Washington

SPARK INNOVATION. CULTIVATE CHANGE.

Yes 3: Download your copy of the Yes Map. The Yes Map is a tool designed to allow you to document your journey, choice points, and strategic decisions and to celebrate key wins. This visual map will serve as an ongoing reminder of key milestones and help you identify new intentions. Fill in your Yes Map, by visiting

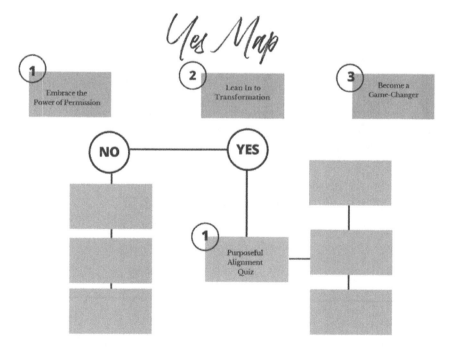

ACKNOWLEDGMENTS

This book is dedicated to all the positive disruptors, movement-builders, frontline activators, healers, weavers, bridge builders, storytellers, provocateurs, historians, innovators, allies, and visionaries who are walking in their purpose and working collectively to tirelessly drive transformational change and innovation at a critical moment in global history. A moment moving us into a movement that will shape a new future, one that has yet to be revealed but will require all of us to play a pivotal role. A moment when the world sees the beauty, strength, and courage of intergenerational leadership shining through, serving as a catalyst for change. An important moment when history compels us to raise our vibrations and intentionally calls us into something bigger than ourselves. A moment when, collectively, systems are interrupted and reimagined.

A heartfelt thanks to my community and collective, who I leaned on heavily throughout my journey and process. Without the help of my philanthropic, nonprofit peers and friends, I wouldn't have remained steady on my path. In particular, Anita Brown-Graham, Mebane Rash, Tara Kenchen, Desiree Adaway, Donna-Marie Winn, Katrina Hutchins, Veronica Hemmingway, Joy Webb, Aundra Wallace, Ashley Shelton, Leslie Winner, the ABFE Women's Leadership family, and countless others.

A special thank you to my CoThinkk team for their love and a soft place to land, in particular Stephanie Swepson-Twitty, Darcel Eddins, Davia Young, Quala Brown, Carolina McCready, Tracy Hopkins, and Lauren Rayburn. To my family, particularly my parents, Yvette and Lonnie Jives, and my siblings, Shauntey and Joe, who offered a listening ear and, when I needed it, painfully honest feedback.

What would I have done without my beta readers, Nicole Townsend, Trista Harris, Gary Hubbell, Ben Barge, Marcus Walton, Jamilla Hawkins, Jehan Shamsid-Deen, and Kristy Tesky? Their honest critique of my manuscript helped ensure I was able to lean in to the lessons learned and provide clarity to support others along this journey.

Finally, my world is better because of the two precious souls I share my life with, my husband, Edmund, and my son, Caleb. Thank you for your support, push, love, truth telling, and commitment. It is my hope that I am able to inspire others to choose purpose and alignment in all aspects of their lives.

ABOUT THE AUTHOR

For more than two decades, Tracey Greene-Washington has led high-level initiatives that address complex issues, earning a reputation as an innovative servant leader inspired by futurism and committed to targeting systemic change, taking risks, and accelerating strategic collaboration. As President of Indigo Innovation Group, Tracey serves as a strategic thought partner, advisor, coach, and consultant to philanthropic, nonprofit, and public and private sectors.

A powerhouse in strategic change efforts, her work amplifies her commitment to accelerating impact through systems-level approaches to achieving equity for communities at the intersection of community economic development, health, education, and leadership development.

In addition to her systems-level work at Indigo Innovation Group, Tracey is the founder of CoThinkk, a social change philanthropy organization committed to shifting the economic mobility, health, education, and leadership narrative of communities of color in Western North Carolina. Affectionately known as Ms. CoThinkk, Tracey is a change strategist who gracefully helps others navigate complex issues and relationships through strategic investments, network building, and civic discourse.

Tracey is also a TEDx speaker and delivered an inspiring talk titled "Addressing Complex Change . . . What If?" as a means to support courageous conversations and solutions to social change. In addition, she is co-owner of a local franchise location, based in Charlotte, North Carolina.

A native of Asheville, North Carolina, Tracey holds a bachelor's degree in social work from the University of North Carolina at Greensboro and a Master of Social Work degree from the University of South Carolina.

She has been lauded for her leadership and work in the philanthropic and nonprofit sector at Kate B. Reynolds Charitable Trust, the Z. Smith Reynolds Foundation, the National Rural Funders Collaborative, and the South Carolina Association for Community Economic Development. Her civic contributions and board service have included NC Early Childhood Foundation, Education North Carolina, the North Carolina Center for Public Policy Research, the Center for Leadership Innovation, and the Southern Rural Development Initiative.

Made in the USA
Columbia, SC
12 November 2020